A Pioneer Church Family

The Autobiography of Pastor Trygve F. Dahle

All scripture is taken from the King James Version of the Bible.

Copyright © 2004 by Mercy and Truth Publishers

All rights reserved. No part of this book may be used or reproduced in any manner whatsoever without written permission of the publisher. For information contact: Mercy and Truth Publishers, 19594 350th Street NW, Newfolden, MN 56738 USA

ISBN 0-9759163-1-9

Printed in the United States of America

Table of Contents

    Introduction
1. My Father 7
2. My Mother 13
3. Graduation, Ordination and First Parish 17
4. The Duluth Parish 21
5. To "Furuly" on Farm Island Lake 23
6. Pioneer Life and Early Childhood
   Recollections 27
7. School Days 33
8. Father's Ministry in Aitkin County
   and Vicinity 41
9. Summer Visitors at "Furuly"—
   The Sverdrups 57
10. More Memories of My Boyhood Days 67
11. We Move to Starbuck 85
12. In the U.S. Navy 97
13. My Years At Augsburg 107
14. My First Parish—Waubay and Tabor 119
15. The Move to Minnesota—Wannaska 133
16. Near the Canadian Border—Hallock 139
17. Our Ministry in North Dakota—McVille 151
18. Our Move to Fargo 165
19. The Lake Region—Spicer, MN 169
20. We Move to Canada 175
21. We Return to Minnesota—LaPorte 183
22. Retirement 189
23. Beginning Again 203
24. No Longer Alone 217
25. Conclusion—In Retrospect 231

Introduction

At various times the last few years I have had friends and relatives tell me that I should write down some of my experiences concerning my youth and my ministry. I too had a strong urge to do the same. I always excused myself by saying, "I'm not a writer."

Even though I was not a writer, through the encouragement of my wife, Anna, in the summer of 1977, I began writing this autobiography. As I would talk about different experiences Anna would tell me, "Now, go and write this down before you forget it." So I had many short anecdotes written on slips of paper.

In the winter of 1984, Anna and I began to put these writings together in a more orderly manner We began with my mother and Dad in Norway; we wrote about their life as immigrants, my dad's ministry, my growing up years and my experiences as a pastor. We continued working on this in the winter of 1985 and 1986.

Our hope is that those who may read this will find it to be both interesting and a blessing to them.

Trygve F. Dahle Sr.

Chapter 1
My Father

I, Trygve Ferdinand Dahle Sr. was born November 14, 1891, in the village of West Duluth, Minnesota, of parents Pastor Ole Dahle, and Regine (Gulbrandsen) Dahle. My father was Pastor of Zion Lutheran Church of West Duluth from 1889–1895. Both my parents came from Norway.

My great-grandfather's name was Ole Olson Orsness, and he married Klara Berte Fyrdsreite, on the Fyrdsreite "gaard" (farm) and took over that piece of property where they made their home. To the best of my knowledge, they had five children, Andreas, (my grandfather), Ingeborg, Jon, Jacob, and Elais. From there, we can trace our genealogy back to "Harald Hârfager," translated, Harald, the Fairheaded. He was responsible for bringing the 32 kingdoms of Norway together into one nation in 872 A.D. This is where Norway's history began.

My grandfather, Andreas Dahle, moved from the Fyrdsreite place to the Dale place, on Dalsfjorden, Sunmore, and dropped the Fyrdsreite name and took the Dahle name. He married Pernille Steinsvik, and to this union six children were born. Rasmine, Johanne, Kanutte, Ole (my father), Peder, and Martinus.

1. Rasmine, married Anders O. Eidseth, and they had four children; 2. Johanne, married Ola Omelfotseter,

and they had four children; 3. Kanutte, married Peter Lillebo and they had four children; 4. Peder, married Anna Bertha Vatne, and had only one child; 5. Ole, married Regine Gulbrandsen in the USA and they had nine children; and 6. Martinus, died young and never married.

Rasmine and Johanne stayed in Norway; Kanutte and Peder went to South Africa, when Great Britain colonized South Africa in the Johannesburg area about 1880–85; and my father, Ole Dahle, came to the USA and attended Augsburg Seminary.

My father was born May 15,1853, and he was only nine years old when his mother died. His father, Andreas Dahle, was a fisherman, and eked out a living for his family from the sea. The nearest place to buy food was Volda, on Voldafjord. They lived at Dalsfjorden which is a small branch of Voldafjord. There were no roads where they lived. The only way to get to Volda, was by boat, and that was about 10 English miles. They also went to church in Volda and it was there that my father was baptized and confirmed. They had to row their fisherman's boat, winter and summer when they went to church or shopping, so they did not get to town very often; as in the summer time it rained quite a bit, and in the winter time, it was cold and snowed, although the fjords were open, and never or very seldom froze over.

They were poor people and when a child, either boy or girl, was 16 years old they had to leave home and find work and make their own way. Their home was hung on a narrow strip of land between the mountain and the fjord. Every place had a couple of cows, a few goats, and sheep, which supplied them with meat, butter, milk, and cheese, and everybody had a potato patch and also raised other vegetables, that they would keep in their "root cellar," dug into the mountain.

The small pasture for the cows and other animals, had to be vacated in the summer time so they could mow it and have hay for the wintertime. So they took their animals up the steep mountain a mile or two where there was a plateau, and plenty of grass for all summer. This they called "Sateren." There they had a little hut for the girl or boy to live in and they also had shelters for the animals. The girl or boy stayed there all summer and tended the cattle and goats, and made cheese and butter which would keep, and was also marketable. There were no roads up to the "Sater," therefore all their needed supplies had to be carried up the mountain and the produce carried down again.

Up on the mountain, there were also several kinds of wild berries, plums and cherries, which had to be harvested at the right time, carried down for household use, and made into jams and juice, etc. It was slim pickings, but they survived. All they had to buy was sugar and flour and coffee; all the rest they raised or got from the sea, or the offspring from the cattle, goats, and sheep. They would exchange a jar of butter or a cheese for the articles they had to buy.

My dad left home when he was 17 years old and went to Alesund. Here he attended a carpenters school "Snikkerskole," to learn the carpenter's trade and also cabinetmaking, "Finsnikkering." He also went to school evenings and studied draftsmanship. When he graduated he went to Kristiansund to look for work. Here he became acquainted with a group of Christian young people and through their influence he came to the assurance of his salvation and began serving his Lord and Savior.

After some time he traveled, taking subscriptions for

a little mission paper and he also held Evangelistic meetings. This took him down the coast of Norway, where he visited nearly every town and village until he got to Kristiansand, which is the southernmost tip of Norway. Nearly every place that he held meetings there were spiritual awakenings. At Ny-Hellesund, nearly all the young people in the town became Christians. A man who operated a Billiard Hall, also was saved and after his salvation he changed his Billiard Hall into a "Bedehus," (prayer chapel).

My father started a Sunday School at Kristiansand. Sunday School was a new thing in Norway. He started out with eight little girls who had been saved and it grew and grew until there were 1100 when he left Norway. At Kristiansand, he also compiled a little songbook which he entitled "Lille Fredsbasun." He sold these little books at his meetings, and the proceeds were enough to pay his fare to America and to keep him at Augsburg the first year.

During his travels, he met several pastors and others, who advised him to go to America and attend Augsburg Seminary. Some of these were K.B. Birkland and Rev. Wettergren. He also had heard of Rev. Georg Sverdrup, from Stavanger, who had been called to teach at Augsburg. At that time Augsburg had only a Preparatory school and Seminary.

In 1881 his decision was made to attend Augsburg, and he embarked from Kristiansand on an old boat for New York. It took them 21 days, and halfway across the Atlantic they encountered a fierce storm from the Northwest, and he became so deathly seasick that he wished he could die, but he did survive and they finally got to New York.

He arrived in Minneapolis on a Sunday night and

school started on Monday morning. When he met Rev. Georg Sverdrup, he said, "Ja, vi faar prove dig, og du faar prove os." (Yes, we will have to try you, and you will have to try us.) Evidently Sverdrup was acquainted with Dad's successful evangelistic work in Norway. It was very difficult for the immigrants, as they came from Norway. They were faced with the task of learning the English language, and besides that, in the Seminary, he had to study the Greek language, but he said that it went well.

In the summer of 1884–85, my father taught "religionsskole," Daily Vacation Bible School at Eagle Lake Lutheran Church north of Willmar, Minnesota. He also worked in the hay and harvest fields for 75 cents a day, thereby earning enough money to continue his education, without interruption.

Most of the students at Augsburg attended Trinity Lutheran Church one and a half blocks from Augsburg. They had a very spiritually active Young Peoples Society, where Professor Sverdrup was also pastor. It was here that my father met my mother, Regine Gulbrandsen. She had come from Norway a year before my father. She was active in Sunday School work at Trinity Church. One of her very best girlfriends had two brothers that were attending the Seminary as well as my dad and they were very much interested in my mother, but my dad won out! My father graduated in a class with 11 others, and they were referred to as the 12 apostles; there was also a special student, which made it 13 and he was called the apostle Paul.

Chapter 2
My Mother

My mother, Regine Gulbrandsen, was born in Magnor, (paa Ostlandet), near Kongsvinger, October 25, 1859. Here she was baptized in Eidskog Lutheran Church and also confirmed there. Her grandfather on her father's side was Gulbrand Nilsen Ingelsrudseter, and his wife, Ranghild Knepperud. They had seven children, five boys and two girls, of whom Grandpa Gulbrand Gulbrandsen, was the next to the youngest. He married Maren Nilsdatter Perkerud, approximately 1856, and they had eight children, five girls and three boys as follows: Marthea, Regine, Anna, Gunerius, Netta (died as a teenager), Olivia, Mentz and Karelius. Marthea married Ole Pederson Gaustadseter, but they later used the name Pearson; Regine, my mother, married Ole Dahle; Anna married Sigvart Gaustadseter; Gunerius married Netta Larson; Olivia came to the USA, worked as a laundress and never married; Mentz married a Swedish girl; Karelius married but had no children.

Marthea, Anna, and Mentz stayed in Norway; Mentz took the name of the home place which was Wangen. Gunerius, Olivia, my mother Regine, and Karelius came to America. Gunerius and Olivia used the name Vang. Karelius said no one could pronounce his name, so he had it legally changed to Charles Wagner. My mother used the name Gulbrandsen until her marriage. There was much confusion in regard to names in Norway and among the immigrants. Some of them chose to use the name of the "gaard," which is the place where they lived, while others chose to use their father's first name and add son to it. Many brothers and sisters, therefore, had different last names.

My mother, Regine, was the second oldest in her family. They lived on the Wangen place, near Magnor, and Grandpa was a "Skogsgubbe," timber man. He bought timber on the stump, cut them down and hauled them to the sawmill and sold them there. They lived on rolling land, heavy timber country, near the Swedish border. They made their living off the timber. Mother said, that in the spring of the year when they first turned the cows out of the barn, they would sometimes stray across the border, so that they would have to go to Sweden to get them for milking. There were few fences at that time.

Grandpa was also a "fiddler," and played at the "folk dances" that were often held in the different homes. When my mother was five years old, she remembers that her father and mother and her grandparents on her mother's side took her along to some laymen's meetings, conducted by the Kasa Brothers, held in the neighborhood. At one of the meetings, both her parents and grandparents were saved. That ended Grandpa's playing for those dances. About two weeks after his salvation, Grandpa took his violin out to the chopping block and made kindling wood out of his violin. He could no longer enjoy his violin which he had used in Satan's service.

My mothers two aunts on her father's side had emigrated to America, and lived at Orrock, Minnesota, near

Big Lake. When Mother was 20 years old, she also came to the USA. It was June 7,1880, when she arrived at her relative's place at Orrock. When she left Norway, she had told her mother that she would be back to visit her in five years. That never materialized although her mother lived to be 92. Very few of the immigrants ever returned to Norway to visit due to family responsibilities, lack of finances, and poor travel conditions. After her mothers death, my mothers desire to return to Norway left her.

After arriving in Orrock, Minnesota, she stayed with one of her aunts for a while, and then went to Minneapolis, and worked as a maid for Pillsbury, one of the owners of the Pillsbury Flour Mills and later for Dr. Dinsmore, a noted physician. She had the privilege to go with her employer, as a maid, to Florida two winters. On one of the return trips, they visited Mammoth Cave in Kentucky. These years that she worked in non-Scandinavian homes were very educational for her. It helped her to learn the English language, proper etiquette and customs and culture of the new world.

Mother came from Norway as a Christian, and after going to Minneapolis she sought out Christian fellowship. She attended Trinity Lutheran Church, which was a block and a half from Augsburg. She joined the Young People's Society and also became active in the Sunday School. Some of her Sunday school pupils were children of the teachers at Augsburg, including the Sverdrups and Oftedals and others. She also helped to organize the first girls mission society in that church.

Like most young people, she had spiritual struggles with doubt and other problems, but she knew where to go; to the Word of God. One time when she was being severely tempted, she cried out to God in prayer, "O

God, give me a word from your Scriptures that will give me Assurance of Salvation." God answered her prayer and gave her 1 John 3:14a, *"We know that we have passed from death unto life, because we love the brethren."* This gave her assurance because she knew that she was the happiest when she was with her Christian friends. This same verse has been a help to me during similar spiritual struggles in times past.

Chapter 3
Graduation, Ordination and First Parish

Father entered Augsburg as a student in 1881, and graduated in 1886. After graduation he accepted a call to the Morris, Minnesota parish. He was ordained June 27, 1886, at the annual meeting of the Conference held at Sand Hill congregation, rural Climax, which is 18 miles southwest of Crookston, Minnesota. The Morris parish consisted of eight congregations and preaching places, namely: Kongsvinger, north of Donnelly; Scandia; Cyrus; Artichoke Lake; Eidskog, east of Ortonville; Beardsley; Browns Valley; and Big Stone City, across the line into South Dakota. Not all of these places had organized congregations, some were only preaching places.

During his student days my father had met my mother at Trinity Lutheran Church and they had become engaged and agreed to be married as soon as he was established in a parish. And so it was, that on July 27, 1886 my father, the Rev. Ole Dahle of Morris, Minnesota and Miss Regine Gulbrandsen of Minneapolis were married in Calvary Lutheran Church in Willmar, Minnesota. The officiating pastor was one of my father's classmates, the Rev. Martin Hegge. Their witnesses were the Rev. E. Gynild and Miss Hegge.

Dad's parish was scattered over four counties. He drove a horse and buggy in the summer and a horse and sleigh in the winter. This involved a lot of driving and there wasn't much time to be at home. He tried to get around to each place at least once in six weeks, but was often hindered in the wintertime because of storms. He would leave home Saturday morning, have the confirmation class in the afternoon; Sunday morning he would have a worship service, baptisms and occasionally Holy Communion. After the morning service they would have a fellowship dinner and in the afternoon he would meet with the Ladies Aid. On Monday he would start for home.

West of Morris there was 50 miles of open prairie, as far as Browns Valley. Many times he was not able to get all the way home, but would have to stop at a farmhouse and wait out the storm. Besides that, there were not many homes along the way. In his own words, he tells about driving one day to Artichoke Lake for a service. "It was the Sunday before Christmas, and it was a beautiful day. The farmers said, they looked for an open winter, but I said, 'it looks like we are going to have a snowstorm. I want to get started for home as soon as possible.' They laughed and said, 'you don't know much about weather in America.' But I started out and got as far as Ole Lofthus. We hadn't more than gotten the horse taken care of when it broke loose, a terrible blizzard from the Northwest. I had to stay there from Sunday night until Thursday morning, before I could get off the place." He said that it was with great difficulty that he got to Morris by noon and that, that same afternoon it started in again from the other direction, for just as many days and that it continued that way from Christmas until Easter. That same winter the Browns

Valley train was blocked all winter. There must have been many anxious hours for my mother as she waited for my father to come home during these storms. There were no telephones or other ways for him to let her know where he was. There was, however, one line of communication that was open and that was to her Heavenly Father. I'm sure she spent much time in prayer for his safe return.

At one of my father's preaching places there was a Danish young man and his fiancée who wanted to get married, but my father wasn't able to get there for three months. The man wanted to go and "get squared" as they said; that is, have a civil ceremony, by the Justice of the Peace, but his fiancée said, "No, we are going to have a Christian wedding." Needless to say, they were overjoyed to see him when he finally got there.

The Kongsvinger Congregation was going to build a church and my father made use of his draftsmanship training, which he had from Norway, and drew the plans for the church. They built after he left and they used his plans, but they made it a little smaller than his plans and they later regretted it as it proved to be too small.

My mother enjoyed their time in the Morris Parish. She wrote in her "Remembrance Book," "After three very happy years among extra delightful and kind people, we moved to Duluth on the recommendation of Professor Georg Sverdrup, where we served two congregations, we had at that time two children, Anker and Astrid."

Chapter 4
The Duluth Parish

Upon a call from Zion Lutheran Church of West Duluth and an encouragement to accept from the Rev. Georg Sverdrup, my father resigned from the Morris parish and accepted the call to the church in West Duluth. Our family moved there in 1889. As far as we can determine he served two churches, Zion in West Duluth and another one in Duluth. The Zion congregation had no building when he came there, but they met in a hall above a saloon. Later they decided to build a church, and my father drew up the plans.

There was much emigration from the Scandinavian Countries to America. Many of the immigrants had settled in the Duluth area. They were fishermen, carpenters, railroad workers and common laborers. These were the people that made up his congregations.

My father had a deep concern for the spiritual welfare of his parishioners. He was a warm-hearted Christian and was concerned that his members had a real experience of salvation. He was a kind and friendly person and was loved by his people. He had a sweet tenor voice and his singing was always a part of his services. It could be said of him, like Mr. Moody said of Mr. Sankey, "He has sung more people into the kingdom, than I could preach in." Father also had a deep insight into the Word of God. His messages were always geared to lead people into full assurance of salvation through Bible studies and prayer meetings. He was a good personal worker, and soul winner. He was faithful in visiting the sick and elderly, and he was a man of prayer.

My mother's brother, Gunerius Vang came from Norway while we lived in Duluth. He was with us some of the time and also with other relatives in the Orrock, Minnesota vicinity. He was married in 1893. He homesteaded four miles south of Deerwood, about 10 miles from where we later settled. It was heavy timber, so he worked to clear the land for planting. The timber was cut and sawed into lumber for the building of homes. All of us children just loved to have Uncle Gunerius come to our house. He was friendly and kind and a real Christian. He was very helpful to us, when we moved from Duluth to Aitkin County. Later on he helped with building fences and many other things.

In the late nineties there was a great depression. It was called the "Panic of the '90s." It hit very hard in the Duluth area. Much of the population lost their jobs. It was the time when Minnesota was opening up for homesteading. My father lost about half of his congregation who went out and took homesteads, mostly in Aitkin and eastern Crow Wing County. He resigned from his churches, after six years in Duluth, and followed his parishioners. Most of them had settled south of Aitkin in heavy timber country.

My father bought the homestead rights from a man who had failed to "prove up" his land. It was about an 80-acre property on the west shore of Farm Island Lake. This property was covered with fine pine timber, white and Norway pine. On this piece of land there was a small log cabin. There was about three quarters of a mile of lakeshore.

Chapter 5
To 'Furuly' on Farm Island Lake

In June of 1895, we made the move from Duluth to Aitkin. Ragna, Trygve (myself), Borghild and Viggo had been born in Duluth. Our family now consisted of six children, besides Mother and Dad; Anker and Astrid were born in Morris. We left Duluth on the Northern Pacific train, going west. The Hinckley fire had started September 1,1894, and had burned all winter, in the underbrush and the large pine trees. It had been an open winter, with no snow, so there was nothing to stop it. As we rode along on the train there was fire along the way on both sides of the tracks, going west from Duluth.

We were met at the depot in Aitkin by one of Dad's former parishioners from Duluth, who had taken a homestead south of Aitkin. He had a team of horses and a wagon with a double-box. The men put the mattresses and quilts and other things that we would need for the first night in the wagon, and we children sat on them. Mother and Dad sat on spring seats with the driver. The fire was still burning and the deeper we got into the woods, the heavier the smoke became. It was becoming difficult to breath, especially for us children, and the driver said he couldn't risk going any further for the sake of the horses either, so it was decided to turn around and go back to the home of the driver where we stayed all night. We found out later that Uncle Gunerius, who was with us, and another man had fought the fire most of the night.

During the night, God sent a heavy rain that quenched the fire except for smoldering logs and stumps. When we awoke the next morning the wind had turned to the northwest, and the air was clear and fresh, and we were able to proceed to our new home, a small log cabin on the lakeshore. Between the log cabin and the lakeshore there was a large pine grove of almost a 100 trees of white and Norway pines. They were from 50- to a 100-feet tall. The Hinckley fire never reached to our property; it had stopped about a mile before it got to our land, so our trees were virgin timber.

When we got to our destination and my mother for the first time viewed the beauty of the landscape at our homestead on the shore of Farm Island Lake, the beautiful mirror-like lake, with its islands, the beautiful pines, and the cabin she said, "Now I feel at home, and this feeling has never left me." No wonder that my dad was inspired to call our place "Furuly" which means pine shelter.

One of the first things my father did after we got settled was to look up his former parishioners who had taken homesteads in the area around the north and east end of Farm Island Lake and south of Cedar Lake. He and several of the men looked over our place and when they saw the small cabin, the men immediately said something had to be done as more room was needed for the pastor and his family. It was decided to leave the log cabin as a kitchen and add a two story frame building to it, south and east. Dad drew the plans and as many of the men were carpenters, they went right to work that summer. Each donated some home sawed seasoned pine lumber, as there were pines in abundance.

The Hanson brothers, Richard and Anton, lived right across the bay south from our cabin. They were fine Christian men and also good carpenters. I also remember a Mr. Johnson, who lived across the other bay east of us. He had two boys, Willie and Charlie, who were teenagers; and Peter Johanson, who had two boys, Arthur and Sigurd and a daughter Clara. They lived on Pine Lake, the first lake east of Farm Island. Mud River flowed through all those lakes. There is a string of five or six lakes east of Farm Island that flowed into Farm Island. They were all spring fed and the inlet was straight south of our place and bordered the land of the Hansons. The outlet went through several other lakes and emptied into the Mississippi River at Aitkin.

These men, and several others, together with my dad worked on the house during the summer to get it closed up before winter came. The kitchen was left as it was, temporarily, and from the kitchen we went east into the dining-living room, and to the left was the master bedroom, in the northeast corner was Dad's office, and the southeast room we called the parlor, which later became a guest room. The front door opened east toward the lake and there we had a good view of the lake and the two smaller islands. My father did most of the inside finishing work. He did it little by little as time permitted. He got sawdust from the saw mill and used that for insulation. Father was a practical man and could figure out ways of doing things to the best advantage.

My father didn't let the work on the house interfere with his ministry. Immediately he began to have informal house meetings, consisting of Bible studies, prayer and fellowship. That first summer they also organized a congregation and since many of the members lived around Cedar Lake and vicinity, they decided to name the congregation, Cedar Lake Lutheran Church. John Holum donated land for the church and the cemetery right across the road from where he lived. My dad drew the plans for the church and construction began that same summer. Some of the charter members were the Carlson Brothers, Edward and Bernhard, they both had large families; the Ed Gustad family; the Rasmussens; Anton and Richard Hanson; the John Holum family; the Peter Johanson family; two Everson families; the John Rom family; the Kristian and Otto Rud families; and several others. All of the members donated lumber and helped build the church. Most of the people walked to church, carrying their Bibles and hymn book, the "Salmebog." Before Dad closed a service he would always sing a good gospel song with a challenging message. He would sing it without accompaniment. All the services were of course in the Norwegian language at this time.

Chapter 6
Pioneer Life and Early Childhood Recollections

Mother was a good gardener, and so one of the first things we did was to get a man with a walking plow, to plow up a garden spot. This was behind the kitchen. Mother had a large garden of vegetables: potatoes, cabbage, carrots, peas, beans, rutabagas, and many other things. I don't remember having tomatoes; they were not a favorite among the Norwegians. They hadn't had them in Norway, so we hadn't learned to like them. We children did the weeding, and how we detested it, but we enjoyed eating it. The garden provided a big portion of our meal. We had a cellar under the kitchen part of the house, with a trap door in the floor where we stored our potatoes and other vegetables in bins on the dirt floor. They kept very well all winter so there was much good eating. Every fall Dad would buy a barrel of good eating apples and that would also be put in the cellar. We children were permitted to eat all the apples we wanted to eat, but if we took an apple we were expected to finish it. We were not allowed to waste them.

The first years we had no well. We used the water from the lake. The lake was sand bottom, and it had both an inlet and outlet and it was before the days of pollution so we had good water. We had a long dock built out into the water about 50 or 60 feet or more, so the water was waist deep where we "dipped" our water for the house. Our neighbor had made us a "bere-tre." The "bere-tre" was made out of a 6-inch spruce log and was carved out to fit on our shoulders and neck, something like a yoke. It was tapered off on each end until it was about 2 inches thick. There we tied a rope with a metal hook on the end so that we could carry two 12 quart pails of water at a time. This we carried up the hill from the lake to the house.

In the winter time when the lake froze over, we chopped holes in the ice. We had one hole where we got water for the house and another hole about a hundred feet away where we watered the cows and horses. Sometimes the holes would drift shut after a snowstorm, and it was difficult to find the waterhole. One time when Father was away, and we had a three day storm, one of the neighbors, John Holum, became concerned about the pastor's family and sent his teenage son, Ed, to see how we were faring. He found the waterhole; he walked right into it and fell in. He was soaked to the waist. He had to change clothes and we boys were too small so our clothes wouldn't fit him, so we gave him some of Dad's everyday clothes to wear, while his clothes dried by the big "potbellied" heater.

In the summer we would catch the rain water that ran off the house. This was kept in barrels and used for washing clothes and other things around the house.

One of the first necessities for our large family was milk. We started out with one cow. We called her "Storebas," because she was a large cow. She was a Holstein and gave lots of milk. She provided us with all the milk and butter that we needed. She was a "fence-buster," and would jump or break through the fences, but Uncle Gunerius helped us build and repair fences. Later on we got a brindle cow, part Guernsey. She gave very rich milk. As time went on, we raised heifers but I don't remember that we ever had more than four cows at a time. There was a small log barn, where we kept the cows. Later, my father built a frame addition to the barn for the horse. He also built a hayloft above both.

Behind the barn, was a small grove of trees and brush. Adolph Stokseth, a "newcomer" from Norway, made his home with us and he began clearing that land. This gave us more land for hay for the animals for the winter. We cut all our hay with a scythe and raked it into shocks by hand with a wooden tined rake, which Dad had made. We raked it into piles to cure and later hauled it to the barn and pitched it into the hayloft. We referred to this hay land as "Adolph's Clearing," as he had done much of the work. Year by year, we cleared a little more until we had nearly 15 acres of hay land.

Adolph became ill while he lived with us. He had an inflammation of the glands in the neck, which they called TB. This illness finally caused his death and it became my father's sad duty to have to write to his mother in Norway informing her about her son's death and funeral. Adolph had come to conscious life in God and had assurance of salvation. This had come about through Father ministering to him.

One year we broke up about a half acre of the hay land and planted corn. As the corn ripened we found out that there were raccoons in the woods and they liked the corn too. They would break down the stalks and eat the corn so we trapped them and ate the meat and sold the pelts.

We cut our own wood for fuel. We would search out dead trees at first and skid them home with our horse,

Maggie, with one end of the log on a "go-devil." This had been made by a neighbor and was an implement used by the lumbermen when skidding the logs over to the loading place. It was almost the shape of an "A" with a crosspiece in the middle, and was generally made from the curved root and stem of a yellow birch. One end of the log was chained to the crosspiece of the "go-devil," this kept the end of the log off the ground and prevented it from digging into the ground as it was pulled along.

Those first years the men of the church helped us with the cutting of the wood and hauling it home. There were no power saws in those days. It all had to be sawed with a crosscut saw so the men often helped us with this, as Father was gone so much of the time on his preaching trips and we boys were too small for this kind of work. This help was greatly appreciated by us. We used the larger chunks in the "potbelly" stove in the living room, and the chunks had to be split into smaller pieces for the kitchen range. Anker and I tried to do some of this sawing and splitting when we were quite young. I remember Mother telling me one time that when Anker was eight and I was four, Anker had complained to her that I was not much help. I can readily understand that was probably true.

Nearly all of our food and living came from our own land. When Father would return from his trips, he would always bring home a few staple groceries, like flour, sugar, coffee, etc. Mother very seldom went to town, maybe two or three times a year, but when she did go she always brought home some special treat. Once I remember in the late summer or early fall, that she brought home one-half dozen pears and she cut them in two and gave each of us children a half. I had never tasted pears before and it was the best fruit I had ever eaten! This part of Minnesota was rich in wild berries. In June, it was strawberries; in July, raspberries; and in August, blueberries. Both the raspberries and blueberries thrived on the burnt over land, which resulted from the "Hinckley Fire." We had to walk a mile to where the fire ended and in this burnt over land there was an abundance of berries. We would take along every available receptacle we could find and always came home with all vessels filled to the brim. I recall one of our best years we canned 100 quarts of strawberries, and about 200 quarts of raspberries and about the same amount of blueberries. The blackberries we ate fresh as they were not as plentiful, but they were very good eating. In the fall we had cranberries. They grew on the moss in our three swamps. There were three kinds of cranberries, one of them we called mossberries. They were a little smaller than the others. We also had some wild plums, pin cherries, chokecherries and June berries.

In the late winter when the snow had settled so there was bare ice on the lake, we would take our sled and a couple of sacks and go to the 40-acre island on the lake which was full of butternut trees. As there were no squirrels on the island and the snow was melted, there on the bare ground lay the butternuts in abundance. We picked them up and filled our sacks and went back home and could have a feast of butternuts, whenever we wanted them. We cracked them on the stumps, and ate the sweet meats.

Farm Island Lake was well filled with fish of all kinds. The only fishing equipment that we had was a spoon-hook and a line that we would pull behind the boat, whenever we rowed to one of the neighbors, on an errand, or to visit Anton Hanson or others across the bay. We always got pickerel, sometimes a walleye or black bass. We always had plenty of fish to eat, and we never took more from the lake than what we could use.

We generally kept a few chickens so we had our own eggs. In the spring we would set a few hens and hatch out baby chicks. These grew up so later in the fall we could have a chicken to eat. One time, my mother sent me out to catch a rooster. I chased him for a long time but couldn't catch him. He finally went into the chicken coop, and I shut the door and went and got my 12-gauge shotgun. I went back to the chicken coop and there he was on the roost with about 15 hens. I picked out the rooster and shot him. The hens fell off the roost too, from fright, but after the dust settled, I picked up my rooster and brought it to Mother and we had a chicken dinner.

In the spring we would buy a couple of little pigs and feed them through the summer and butcher them in the fall when the weather got cold enough so that the meat would keep as we had no refrigerator or deep freeze in those days. Some of the meat we salted down or canned. Sometimes we would have a calf to butcher also. One of our neighbors was a good butcher and he helped us with this.

We also had wild game that we used for food. Rutted grouse was our favorite and the easiest to get as they were quite tame. Occasionally we would get a duck. We never shot just for sport but it was for food. God supplied us with our food as we pray in the Lord's Prayer, "Give us this day our daily bread."

Chapter 7
School Days

We had about two miles to walk to our school, which was called the Caza Schoolhouse. It was a one-room log building, which was heated by a wood burning homemade stove. The wagon road was about five miles, but we had a shortcut, a path along the lakeshore, through the woods, and over a "Corduroy," two logs parallel, laid end-to-end, over a swamp, a floating bog, about one-quarter of a mile long. When it froze up in the fall, we would walk on the ice about one and one-half miles and the rest of the way through the woods to the school house.

When we walked on the path through the woods, Astrid, our oldest sister, in the upper grades, would tell us a continued story, which was very fascinating. She was blessed with a very vivid imagination and kept the rest of us spellbound with her story. Often, I would be first in line, as there were ruffed grouse, which were very tame; so I would throw my baseball or a stone at it and was successful hitting them occasionally, knocking them out, and then I would run over and ring it's neck, and put it in my bag, and take it home. They were very good eating. Later when I grew older, I would carry the 12-gauge, single-barreled shotgun, and the year I was 11 years old I shot eleven partridges, as we called the ruffed grouse. I shot some of them going to and from school.

At school, we played many games at recess like, pump-pump-pull away, duck on a rock, one old cat, and other games. Right in front of the schoolhouse were two big white pines almost 100 feet tall with big branches. My pal, Oscar Malvik, and I were the same age and we did things together. Often we would climb these two trees, to the top. It would take us about 10 minutes to climb up and about the same time to come down and recess was only 15 minutes, so we came late for class; which of course aggravated our teacher. One time, she was going to punish us two boys and she took Oscar first. She took him out of his seat, shook him, threw him on the floor and kicked him. Then she came to me and I hung onto the top of desk, and the top came off, so I had to let go and then she swung me around and I caught hold of the end of the blackboard and that came off the wall, so she left me alone and sat down and cried; poor thing. I put the blackboard back on the nail and went to my seat and put the top back on my desk and tried to study. This, of course, did not happen every day. We did not try to be mean, but we were not always kind to our teacher, shame on us. One of the reasons we came in late that recess was that we felt our teacher had unjustly punished us one other time for something we had not done. She had kept us in at another recess and we felt we had been cheated out of our recess time.

We had eight grades in our school and the term was eight months. As time went on, a German family moved into the community and this man was elected to the school board. He felt that only six grades were needed but the others would not agree to that; however, he was able to influence the board to cut the school to seven months. Borghild and I were in the eighth grade and when we came to the end of the seven months in the

Casa school; we felt that we needed that extra month and there was another school across the lake, where they had eight months and also a very good teacher. We decided to go there to finish out our grade so we could take a State examination, which was required for graduation.

We walked to that school across the lake, as long as it was frozen over. When spring came and it started to thaw from the shore and out, there got to be an open space of about 100 feet. l had a duck canoe, which was light, and Borghild and I got in the canoe and paddled over to the ice and I got out onto the ice and pulled the canoe up on the ice so that Borghild could step out. Then we walked across the lake, pulling the canoe behind us until we got to the other edge of the ice. We then put the canoe back in the water; I helped Borghild to get in and we paddled to the shore. From there we walked about a quarter of a mile to the school house. This was repeated morning and night until the term was completed.

After the school was out, we were ready to take the final tests sent out by the state. It was required to have a passing grade in all subjects. I passed all my subjects with flying colors, except grammar, which proved to be my "Waterloo." I failed in grammar, but received a grade of 100 in arithmetic and good grades in history and geography. Borghild passed in all her subjects.

Very few of the young people, especially boys, went to school beyond the eighth grade. They had to go out and get work to help support the family. The most common work was the logging camps in the winter, the "drives" in the spring, and the harvest and threshing in the Dakotas in the fall. Most of the people had a long way to go to get to a high school and, of course, there were no cars or school buses. Those that did go to high school stayed in town and the girls were able to work for their room and board.

Our parents valued education and wanted us to get as much as we could. Money was scarce, but as we got older, we helped each other. When Astrid, my oldest sister, finished the eighth grade she got a permit to teach and she taught country school. Astrid was a very sincere Christian and wherever she taught, she started up Bible classes among young people and also their parents. Many people came to a saving knowledge of Jesus Christ through her efforts. She was a very outgoing person. Later on she attended State Normal School, both at Duluth and Moorhead.

Ragna had a call from God to be a missionary from a very young age. Pastors and missionaries who came to work with Dad on deputation made their home with us. They had a great influence on our young lives. The cause of missions was kept alive for us constantly through our daily devotions and contacts with workers on the mission field. Ragna went to high school in Aitkin. She worked for a family and received board and room. After high school, she taught in the country schools, saved her money and later went to State Normal School.

Anker didn't have an opportunity to go to high school, but he had a hunger for further education. This became a concern for the family. His desire was to go to Augsburg. At that time Augsburg had what was called Preparatory and Theology. Preparatory was three years of preparation for the Seminary. The Preparatory was a combination of high school and college subjects. The problem was, "How could this be financed?" Father and Mother and the rest of us had a family discussion. We decided, "We have a lot of good pine timber on our land. How can we convert this into money?" It was agreed that Anker and I would take out 50,000 feet of logs and haul them to Kibby's sawmill, which was across the lake and past the 40-acre island. There it would be sawed into lumber and sold and this was Anker's school money. We cut most of the logs on Mother's north forty, which she had bought with her inheritance money from Norway when her father died.

This was no small task for two young boys. Anker was about 19 and I was four years younger. We worked at it all winter, in knee deep snow. First we picked out a tree and had to decide which way we wanted it to fall, so it wouldn't get hung up in the other trees. We used a two-man crosscut saw to fell it and then we cut it into 10- or 12-foot lengths, depending on the straightness of the tree. We used our team of horses to skid the logs down to the lakeshore, where we had two long skids that we rolled the logs on, so they would be ready to load onto the sled to be hauled across the lake to the sawmill. We waited to do this until the snow was gone off the lake and the ice was bare. We had to make use of the time to get the hauling done while the ice was still solid. We had only about two weeks to do this before the ice would weaken.

We would often see timber wolves on the lake. They generally hung around one of the small islands in the direct route to the sawmill. One day when Anker was coming home from the mill, with his sled empty to get another load, he was chased by one of these wolves. He had nothing in the sled, except the bunks, not even an axe. He made the horses run and as he got closer to the shore there was a man with a gun, who began to shoot at the wolf and he was scared off. This was a scary experience for Anker.

One time a little later, I had a similar experience. After the logs had been sawed into lumber, we had to haul it to Aitkin to sell it. When I drove past the island I always looked carefully to see if there were any wolves and this morning I saw one standing on the island. When I got as close as I dared, he was still standing there. I had my old 44 rifle and I took aim and shot him. I tied him to the sled and drove on to the mill where I loaded up my lumber, threw the wolf on the top of the load and drove on to Aitkin. This created quite a stir in town when I drove in with my wolf. I was the envy of the other young men. This was profitable also, as I got $15 in bounty from the state and another $15 for the hide. So much for the wolf. We had to get the hauling done while there was good sleighing and we could use the winter roads. These went across the lakes and sloughs and avoided the hills.

This is the way that we got Anker's school money. It totaled $300. Father thought maybe the money should be used to pay up the grocery bill, as he never wanted to have debts. Mother didn't like debts either, but she said, "This is Anker's school money." The first thing that Anker did was to go to Aitkin and buy clothes, including his first store-bought suit. It was a Hart-Schaffner-Marx product. I still remember how handsome and "sharp" he looked in his new suit.

Anker took a train to Minneapolis, and there he entered Augsburg. When he registered for school Professor Sven Oftedahl, who was the registrar, said, "Jasaa Dahle, du skal gaa paa Augsburg?" and Anker answered, "Ja, men jeg vil ikke bli Prest.", to which the old Professor remarked, "Nei, langt ifra Dahle, det maa du ikke ble, utn du maaa." ("So you are going to

Augsburg?" "Yes, but I am not going to be a preacher." "Of course not Dahle, that you must never be, unless you have to.") These last words, "unless you have to," Anker never forgot. They stuck and Anker had to become a preacher. The Lord kept calling him until he said yes and he served his Lord as a pastor in the LFC until his retirement.

After Anker left for school, the full responsibility for the work around home fell on me, as I was then the oldest boy at home. This I did not consider a hardship as I loved manual labor, rather than books. I liked to do things with my hands and I enjoyed the great outdoors. I always said, "I would rather haul manure than read a book." Viggo, who was three years younger than I, now became my helper. He and I were very close and did things together. He also loved the outdoors and we hunted and fished together. He helped me with the work that required two people, like getting the hay in the barn and other things.

In 1911, Father received a call to serve two churches in Starbuck, Minnesota. After we moved there, the younger children all had opportunity to attend school, including high school, thus the school problem was solved.

Chapter 8
Father's Ministry in
Aitkin County and Vicinity

Cedar Lake Lutheran Congregation was his home base. He had also established a congregation at Deerwood, where Mother's brother, Gunerius Vang, was a charter member. These were the two congregations that were the closest to where we lived. From here he reached out in all directions looking up homesteaders of Scandinavian descent. For a long time, he was the only Lutheran pastor in the whole area. He traveled in Crow Wing, Aitkin, Carlton, Beltrami and surrounding counties. At one time he had as many as 45 preaching places, this included homes, schoolhouses, town halls, logging camps and he also visited in the jails. He went wherever there were people. Because of the number of places that he went, he didn't get around to each place more than every five or six weeks.

My father was ordained in 1886, in the Norwegian-Danish Conference, referred to mostly as "the Conference." In 1890, there was a merger of this synod with two other small Scandinavian synods. In the new synod, there were two distinct tendencies, which became evident very soon. One was the "High Church" tendency, which wanted to pattern the church in America after the State Church in Norway. They had a strong emphasis on liturgy, with the predominance of the clergy over the laity. They discouraged any lay activity, like Bible studies or free prayer. The other tendency was the opposite. It was "Low Church." They used very little liturgy, and they said, the only authority over the congregation was the Word of God and the Holy Spirit and that the pastor was to be a servant of the congregation. They encouraged lay activity, prayer meetings and Bible studies. They also stressed personal salvation of the individual. Augsburg Seminary with Professors Georg Sverdrup and Sven Oftedal, as it's leaders sided with the Low Church element. My father agreed with Sverdrup and Oftedal and became a part of "Augsburg's Friends" until the Lutheran Free Church was formed in 1897. He was affiliated with the LFC the rest of his life.

Father did not stress the organizing of congregations, although many of his preaching places later became congregations. His calling was to preach the saving gospel wherever he went. There are many souls in heaven today, as the result of his ministry. He had a special gift of leading his listeners into a saving knowledge of Jesus Christ. He had a simple message, but he brought it in a warm, loving way. He not only preached the gospel, but he lived it as well. He was loved and welcomed wherever he went.

We had many fine laymen in Cedar Lake Congregation who conducted services when Father was gone, so we had Sunday school and a worship service almost every Sunday. It was a special treat for us to have him home with us for a weekend. I can still see him in my mind's eye as he stood at the pulpit with his eyes uplifted as he prayed just as if he could see the one to whom he was praying. I can hear him now as he quoted from memory the first few verses of Isaiah 40, in

A Pioneer Church Family

Norwegian, of course. "Troster, troster mit folk, siger eders Gud." His sermons were filled with scripture quoted from memory. He had memorized hundreds of choice verses which enriched his messages which were all geared to leading his listeners to full assurance of salvation.

Father had a lyric, tenor voice, which he made good use of in his services. At home also, when we had our family devotions, he would lead us in singing many songs. Sometimes, he would sit down at the organ. He could not play by notes, but he could accompany himself by chording any song he wanted to sing. At other times he would sit in his chair, with his songbook and sing one song after another. Mother also liked to sing, although she did not sing solos. This gave us children all a love for music.

Some of Dad's preaching places, besides Cedar Lake and Deerwood were: Bay Lake, on the way to Deerwood; McGregor; Kimberly; Thor, south of Kimberly; Tamarack; Carlton; Cloquet; Moose Lake; Brainerd; Long Lake, south of Brainerd; Pequot; Little Falls; Walker; Bemidji; Crosby; Cass Lake, and many more in the surrounding area. He had many house meetings and had key homes in the various areas where they met. In the summertime, he would often have the service in the open air on the lawn of the farmstead. This gave opportunity for a larger group to gather. One time, Borghild and I went with Dad to an afternoon meeting at a home south of Deerwood. It was a beautiful sunny afternoon and I remember she and I sat under a plum tree, full of ripe plums, and while Dad was preaching we helped ourselves to some of the fruit.

On another one of Dad's trips I was with him. He was to preach in Deerwood on Sunday morning and this was Saturday afternoon. We were to stay that night at the home of one of my father's many Swedish friends who lived about three miles south of Deerwood. When we drove into the farmers yard he met us and took the horse to put him in the barn where he could be fed and watered. He told us to go the house where his wife met and welcomed us. Before going in the house, the farmer said "Maybe the pastor would like a sack of oats for his horse." Father said, "Yes, I'm getting a little low on feed and I will gladly accept the gift." The farmer said, "Trygve, maybe you will come and hold the sack while I fill it." Dad went in the house and I went with the farmer. He took one of his tall grain sacks and we went to the granary. He gave me the sack to hold while he scooped oats into it. When I thought it was full, I gathered the top together to close it and he said, "Don't be in a hurry." He took the sack and bounced it up and down a few times and put in two more scoops. Now, I thought surely it was full, but he said, "wait a minute" and he bounced it some more and put in a third scoop— I was amazed. Then he took the top of the sack and closed it very carefully and the grain was running out on all sides, he then took a twine and tied it. You could not get another handful of grain into it. That sack was full and I mean full.

I have often though of this experience and used it as an illustration in my sermons. It reminds me of the words of Jesus in Luke 6:38. *"Give, and it shall be given unto you; good measure, pressed down, and shaken together, and running over, shall men give into your bosom. For with the same measure that ye mete withal it shall be measured to you again."* Down through the years, we have seen, how God has literally fulfilled this promise, time and again. He has supplied our every need according to his riches in glory in Christ Jesus.

Father drove a horse and buggy in the summertime; and in the winter the horse and a single sleigh, called a cutter. When the snow got deeper, he would ride horseback; and when it got deeper yet, he traveled on skis. I can see him yet, starting out on Saturday afternoon on his skis; his satchel strapped on his back, a strong cord tied to the point of each ski. This cord went over his shoulders so that going up hill he could just step off the skis and pull them along as he walked up the steeper hills and going down hill, the cords helped him to keep his balance. In his satchel, he had his Bible, hymn book, his pastors handbook, the Communion elements, some handkerchiefs, his nightshirt, etc.; he needed no razor, as he had a full beard. It gave us children a lonesome feeling, to see him go, as we knew he would be gone over Sunday and come back Monday or Tuesday, depending on the circumstances. He wore a fur coat and good mittens, but keeping his feet warm was a problem.

In one community, as he was visiting homes, he stopped at one place and he was met at the door by the lady of the house. After he had introduced himself as a Norwegian Lutheran pastor; she burst into tears and said, "You are the first pastor, I have seen since I left the 'old country'!" Could you have a meeting tonight? I will send the children out to invite the neighbors."

Needless to say, he was happy to do that, and the house was filled with people, mostly women and children, as their husbands were away working in the logging camps. After the service, he baptized several children, started a confirmation class and a Ladies Aid. This group later formed a congregation.

Many of Dad's preaching places could only be reached by train, because of the distance. The Northern

Pacific train came from Duluth and went west through Aitkin and Deerwood in the morning, and another train came through in the afternoon, going east. If Dad was going to McGregor, Kimberly or Tamarack, he would take the afternoon train from Aitkin; but if his destination was Brainerd or west, he would get the morning train to Deerwood, which was closer. One of us would take him to the train.

I can remember the first time that I took Dad to the train all by myself. He was going to Brainerd. I was about nine years old and we drove to his church at Deerwood; tied the horse to the hitching post behind the church, and Dad and I walked down to the depot where he was to board the train. He bought his ticket and we stood on the platform waiting for the train. Then we heard the whistle, and saw the train coming around the bend. The train stopped, Dad got on, and the train pulled away, and I stood on the platform. I never felt more alone in all my life, than I did at that time. I could not keep the tears back—Dad was gone, and I was alone. I walked back to "old Maggie," crying, hugged her, and cried some more, and she seemed to understand and comforted me. Then I hitched her to the buggy and started for home. Now the tears were gone and we were on our nine-mile trip homeward. I was myself again.

Maggie was also glad to go home. It was easy to get her to run when we were going home, but going away from home she often limped pitifully. She did have a little spavin in one of her hind legs, which would always show up when we were going away from home, but seemed to be forgotten when homeward bound.

Pioneer work was hard but the people were open to the gospel. The homesteaders and newcomers were poor people. This was a time of economic hard times and money was scarce. This also affected the pastor. Later on, he received some help from the Home Missions Department of the Lutheran Free Church. This was a great encouragement.

Some fruit of Dad's ministry was the Petraborg Brothers, who had a grocery and general merchandise store in Aitkin. They were very kind to Dad and his credit was always good. He could get groceries whenever he needed to but in time, of course, it had to be paid, so whenever he got some money, he would apply it on the bill.

Father had no set salaries at any of his preaching places, but this did not stop him from serving them. As they were able, they did from time to time, give him an offering. He also received gifts for ministerial acts, baptisms, weddings, funerals, etc. Some time after 1900, Deerwood Congregation promised him $30 a year and some time later the Cedar Lake Congregation, also called Dorris Congregation, gave him $50 a year.

At one community, north of Cedar Lake, he had been serving for several months and had received no remuneration. The women were concerned about this situation and were talking together about what they could do to help. They decided, "Let us each one bring a little milk and get together and make a cheese for the pastor. He will be here next Sunday." So that is what they did, and when Father came the next Sunday, the happy women presented him with a large cheese as a gift for his services, which he gratefully and cheerfully accepted.

Father also ministered to those who had been locked up in jail. He was a good friend of the sheriff in Aitkin County and whenever someone had been put in jail the sheriff would let my father know about it. There were saloons in those days, this was before Prohibition.

Alcohol was the cause of most of the arrests. Many of the men were away from home, working in the logging camps in the wintertime and when they came home with their hard earned money they would yield to temptation and stop in the saloon thinking they would just have one drink, but it usually got to be many more—one drink led to another.

One couple had agreed that when the husband came home in the spring, they were going to use some of the money and buy a screen door. The wife had been wanting this for a long time so they could keep the flies out of the house during the summertime. It turned out so that the saloonkeeper got the money and the wife had to wait another year for the screen door.

When Father visited these men in jail they were a penitent lot. They hadn't planned to get drunk, get in a brawl and end up in jail, but alcohol had gotten the best of them. Father would share the Word of God with them and try to lead them into a better life—a new life with Jesus, who could give them victory over these sins.

One of the hardest experiences, my father had to go through was to be in attendance at the execution of a man who had been sentenced to death by hanging for the murder of his own daughter. This man had lived about 10 miles east of us and after his wife's death, in his grief, he had taken to drink. One time when he came home, still under the influence of alcohol, he became angry with his oldest daughter and stabbed her to death.

Father visited him in jail several times and showed him from scripture that there was forgiveness even for this crime. This was hard for the man to believe, but in time he was able to accept God's forgiveness. He requested my father to be with him at his execution and Father promised that he would do this. When everything was ready and he was on the stand with the noose about his neck the sheriff asked him if there was anything he wanted to say. He said, "Yes, alcohol is the cause of this terrible act. If I had been sober I would never have done such a thing. I loved my daughter. My friend, Rev. Dahle, has proven to me, through the Bible, that there is also forgiveness for this terrible crime." As he pleaded with the men not to drink, but to get right with God, many of the spectators were weeping. After his testimony, the execution proceeded and his soul went immediately to Jesus his Savior.

There was no employment for the men in the wintertime, except to go away from home and work in the Logging Camps. Many of my father's parishioners also worked in these camps. There were also many men who were transients that worked in these camps in the winter; on the "drives" in the spring, when they floated the logs down the river; and in the harvest fields of North Dakota in the summer. Many of these transients were a bad influence on the men that came from our homes and families out of the congregation.

Weyerhauser had several of these logging camps in the north woods and they had built temporary railroad tracks off the main line into the heart of their logging operation. Here they could load the logs right onto the flatcars and haul them to the sawmills in Minneapolis and other places.

These men were away from their homes and churches, therefore, Father felt the need to go to them where they were. As time and strength permitted, he visited these camps. The only way to get there was to get on these slow moving logging trains. These trains never stopped completely, so he would have to step up on the last car which was the caboose.

On one such trip, there was a man, with a whiskey jug also trying to get on the train. He was trying to get up the steps but was also concerned about getting his whiskey jug along, which he was almost losing. After he got on the train it was Dad's turn. As Dad tried to get on, this man with the jug was lying in his way. Dad got one hand on the handrail and with his suitcase in the other hand, he was able to get one foot on the step, but could get no further until this other man got out of his way. The train gave a lurch and the man rolled over, so there was room for Dad to get on. This man could have reached out his hand and helped Dad get on the train, but then he would have had to let go of the whiskey jug which he was trying so desperately to save.

Father had visited this camp before so many of the men recognized him when he came. The man with the jug, evidently recognized him also, and knew that he was a pastor. He wanted the pastor along! After they arrived at the camp, the man said to the men, "Have a drink, men. We have a preacher along. There's going to be a meeting tonight." Father did have a meeting. Many of the men were of a rough element, but they listened to the message from the Word of God, respectfully. At the close of the meeting, there were many decisions for the Lord. Many of these men who were away from their families, had also drifted away from their God; and now, they, like the prodigal, chose to come back to the Lord, and back to their homes; a better husband and father. After these meetings, the men would pass the hat and give Dad an offering. Sometimes these offerings were better than the ones he received at his regular preaching places.

The Confirmation classes from our home churches, Cedar Lake and Deerwood, often met at our home; and

I can remember, seeing them come walking, some from 10–15 miles away. There were no 12 year olds; they were from 16 to 20 years old, mature young people. I was 16 when I was confirmed. Borghild and I were confirmed together. Dad sought always to bring his classes to a real experience of Salvation. I can remember when I was "reading for the minister," which was my father; I want to tell you, I had to know my lessons, which included choice scripture verses from the Word of God. This Word of God really convicted me of sin. I had never committed any of the outward, openly, coarse sins such as drinking, dancing, smoking, swearing, etc., but a sinner?—yes.

I can remember how, while doing chores out in the barn, I would go up in the hayloft and bury myself in the hay so no one could see or hear me and as I wept before the Lord, I confessed my sins and asked for forgiveness. 1 John 1:9 says, *"If we confess our sins, he is faithful and just to forgive us our sins, and to cleanse us from all unrighteousness."* I acted on the first part of the verse, as I had confessed my sins, but I didn't act on the second part and accept the forgiveness personally; in other words, I took my burden to the Lord, but I didn't leave it there. If I would have told my dad or mother about my feelings I could have gotten help.

My sins were not gross sins, but sin is not what we do, but what we are. In the Confession of Sin, we confess, "I am by nature sinful and unclean—" That is what we are born with. That is the, "old nature," also called the "old man." When God forgives us our sin, we are saved, and receive a "new nature." These two natures are always at war and the battleground is our hearts. The Devil, our arch enemy, works through our old nature and God works through our new nature. God calls to us and invites us to open our hearts and let Him come in and live in our hearts (see Rev. 3:20). The Devil wants us to live for the world. On whatever side we cast our vote, that side wins in the battle.

That going over from a child's faith, which Dr. Hallesby calls, "unconscious life in God," to adult faith or "conscious life in God," can be very hard; nigh unto the experience of the conversion of a hardened sinner. Some people call this experience, a "born again experience." We, who have been baptized as infants, believe and teach that we are "born again" in baptism; however, sooner or later we have to have this awakening of sin in our hearts, which we were not conscious of as infants and small children.

I can remember, Ludvig Hope, telling of his struggle, when he became conscious of sin in his life. When he heard about some revival meetings in his neighborhood, he would go, hoping to get converted. Others were saved, but not Ludvig. He was "reading for the minister" at that time. He went to several meetings like that, but nothing happened to him, so he concluded that he was too big a sinner, so there was no salvation for him.

One day, when he was weeding the garden and studying his Catechism at the same time, he read in the second article, "He has redeemed me, a lost and condemned creature—" He stopped and said, "What did I say? He has redeemed me?" Then the light dawned upon him, that Jesus had redeemed him—not with silver or gold, but with His holy and precious blood (see 1 Peter 1:18–19). He began to pray and thank God there in the garden. This gave Ludvig peace, the peace for which he had been seeking.

So also with me, I too found peace, when it became clear to me, that what Jesus had done for me was enough. There was forgiveness for even me. When the Word of God is taught in all its purity, the Holy Spirit uses the Word to convict us of our sins (see John 16:8) and the only one who can take it away is Jesus.

Father had many and varied experiences in his ministry. Some of them proved to be a great blessing to him and he often talked about them.

One such experience happened in our home church, Cedar Lake Lutheran Church. It was a Sunday morning and he was having a Communion service. When the communicants came forward, he noticed a certain man come forward whom he knew was not a confessing Christian and he had never gone to Communion before, therefore Father wondered, shall I give him Communion or shall I pass him by? Father prayed that God would give him guidance as to what he should do. Father thought, what would Jesus do? He finally decided to give him Communion. The man was weeping during the distribution of the elements. After the service the man talked to Dad and said, "I'm sure you wondered why I came to Communion, but I wanted to accept Jesus as my Savior and I didn't know of any better way to come." This gave Dad great joy, and he was glad that he hadn't passed him by. This experience brought this man into a real living relationship with Jesus and from then on he was one of Dad's best Christian men in the congregation.

One of our neighbors had a son by the name of Dan. He was about 17 years old. They were an unchurched family and this boy had lived an ungodly life. One day his father came to Dad and told him about his son, Dan's death. We didn't know about it, but he had been ill for quite some time, possibly Tuberculosis or some other respiratory disease. The night that he died, it was a perfectly still evening, no wind, but just as Dan died, he screamed, and a sound as of a rushing wind went through the house and every door flew open. After that it was perfectly still again. It was just as if the hosts of Hell had come to claim his soul. This was such a terrifying experience for the father as he related it to my father. Father had an opportunity to pray with him, which resulted in his salvation.

There was another family that lived about five miles further east. Dad had a preaching place there and the mother in that family was a wonderful Christian. This woman became sick and died. Some of her teenage children told my father that the morning that she died, they saw a team of beautiful white horses in the yard, close to the window of the room where she lay. There were no white horses anywhere in the community. It would seem, that God had given them a vision, as an assurance, that their mother had been taken home to the Lord.

Father had his office in the northeast corner of our house. There he had his library and also his desk with many drawers, a cot where he could rest, and a little wood-burning heater which he used when the weather was cold. This was "forbidden territory" for us children. When he was in there studying, we were not allowed to come in, unless we knocked, and he said "come in." I remember once, I forgot and went in without knocking. When I opened the door, there was Dad on his knees by his office chair. I closed the door very quietly and tiptoed back out. It made quite an impression on me.

Many years later, after I was in the ministry, my family and I were on vacation. We went home to my folks at "Furuly." My father and I went to get the mail, about a mile away. As he and I were walking, Father said, "Come Trygve, I will show you my little prayer chamber." We took a detour off to the right, into the heavy underbrush, and there was an open spot. He showed me a little knoll where the brush was hanging over on all sides, this was his prayer chamber. The evidence was there that it had been used often. Needless to say, we knelt, and prayed together. It seemed as if heaven was open to us, which indeed it was.

The Lord gave Father a very fruitful ministry. In later years, after I myself was in the ministry, I would often meet people who had known my father and they would tell me how he had been a blessing to them in one way or another.

Chapter 9
Summer Visitors at Furuly—The Sverdrups

When Professor Georg Sverdrup, President of Augsburg Seminary, heard that my father had moved from Duluth to Aitkin County, he visited us several summers, from the last of June to the first of August. I don't recall which years, but it must have been the last years of the "nineties."

On his first trip he came alone. That year he brought a 16-foot round-bottomed row boat, as a gift for Dad. We had no boat until that time. Dad named the boat, "RATATUSK." I do not know where he had picked up that name. Dad, who had done a lot of sailing in Norway and also was a carpenter, added two or three inches to the keel, and a sail with a 12-foot mast, with a main sail and a foresail, put on a rudder, and we sailed, instead of rowed, when the weather was suitable. It saved a lot of hard work. We used to sail and troll for northerns, who like a fast moving bait. If we trolled for walleyes we would row slowly. There was plenty of fish of all kinds so we were always well supplied with fresh fish, especially after Sverdrup came, who loved to fish and also liked to eat them. He was on the lake every day if it was not stormy.

When he first came, he asked my mother when she needed the fish for dinner, and she gave him a certain hour and from then on, Sverdrup always came with his catch, cleaned and ready for the frying pan and on time. He was never late for a meal. Mother fried or baked the fish and also made fish balls and fish soup. It was delicious.

The second summer, Sverdrup came again and this time he had another row boat along, a 14-footer, the same kind as the first one. This was his boat that he used when he was fishing, but we could have free use of it too, when he was not using it, and we kept it in store for him. We children liked Sverdrups boat, as it was lighter and easier to row and especially to turn around, after Dad had put the deeper keel on the 16-footer.

Every year we would build a dock about three feet wide and about 30 feet long. It had to be taken up every year after it froze up as the ice would destroy it if we didn't. At the end of the dock, the water was about three feet deep, so Mother warned us, especially the younger ones, to be careful and not fall off the dock and not to go too far out when swimming.

One day Sverdrup was walking out on the dock, looking back at something on the shore, and stepped off the end of the dock where the water was about waist deep. Mother laughed and said that she had warned the children to be careful and not fall off the dock, but it never entered her mind to warn Sverdrup.

One summer when Sverdrup, Viggo, and I were walking along the lakeshore and were talking, Sverdrup asked me if I would stand on my head and I said, "Sure." "Will you stand on your head for me? I'll give you a nickel." So I stood on my head. Sverdrup laughed and gave me the nickel. I had to do many stunts for him. Sverdrup liked little boys and we liked him.

One summer late in June we were sitting in our park,

as we called it; seven large pine trees, in a perfect circle, where Dad had put a wood chunk by each tree, and a wide pine board on the chunks as seats. We had room for the whole family and more. Between the two closest trees we had no board, that was the entrance. Then we had a table in the middle where we often had our noon or evening meals during the summer. While we were sitting there, all of a sudden, a livery rig appeared, coming in full trot, and stopped in our yard. Who should step out but Sverdrup, his wife and two youngest daughters. That was a surprise for us.

After greetings, the baggage unloaded and the livery rig gone, Sverdrup handed Mother a large paper bag. "This is a treat for the children," he said. It was a big bag of candy. I had never seen such a big bag of candy before. It must have been 50 cents worth. Of course, Mother knew better than to turn the bag over to us, but she opened the bag, and gave us all a treat, and then put the bag away where only she knew where it was. She took it out and gave us all a treat every day and that bag lasted almost all summer.

Then Sverdrup gave Mother two cotton sailor suits. "These are for Trygve and Viggo," he said. Then it was Mrs. Sverdrup's turn and she had some dresses and other things for the girls. The Sverdrups always brought some presents when they came. After that, Sverdrup lost no time changing clothes and getting his little boat to go fishing. How they enjoyed the quietness of this "wilderness paradise," by the lake which Sverdrup called the "Pearl of Minnesota." There was no one living beyond us, it was the end of the road. The livery rig had to go back the way he came for four miles, before he got on the Post Office road that went to Aitkin. We got our mail once a week. Later on, it was twice a week. Our nearest neighbor was a mile and a half south along the lakeshore. The only way to get there was by boat or walking on a path along the shore, so we had absolute privacy. Sverdrup loved this privacy and could have a good rest.

Viggo and I loved to walk and talk to Sverdrup. One day we were all dressed up in our new sailor Suits. We were walking among the trees talking and we came to a little tree about six inches in diameter and Sverdrup asked me if I could climb that tree? I replied in the affirmative, and he said, "Will you climb that tree for me?" "Yes," I was game, so up I went. When I was up about six feet, he said, "O, that is high enough, you had better come down now." Coming down, and when I was near the ground, I dropped down; but a little sharp twig caught the leg of my new suit and tore it, and also punctured the skin, so the blood ran down my leg. I said, "Det har gaat hul paa mig," (My skin has been punctured.) Sverdrup chuckled and said, "Ja, det er ikke saa farlig med skinne, det vekser snart igjen, del er verre med boksa." (It is not so bad about the skin, that will soon heal, but it is worse with the pants.) Mother took care of both in short order.

Sverdrup and Dad planned to build a bathhouse where we could change our clothes when we went bathing. Dad said he had some lumber at the sawmill across the lake, about three miles, but to get it home was the problem. Being it was not too many boards, he thought maybe they could use both boats and lay the lumber across both boats, each row his own boat, and that way get the lumber home without getting it wet. Ordinarily we would make a raft of the lumber and tow it home behind the boat. One day when the weather was calm he asked Sverdrup if he was willing to try that.

Yes, he was willing, so off they went, got to the mill, loaded the lumber across the back part of both boats and started home. All went well until they neared the Island, about halfway, a wind came up, and the waves swamped Sverdrup's boat, so he came crawling on all fours on the lumber over to Dad's boat, but the extra load, and with the waves getting bigger, it swamped Dad's boat too, so they had to shove the lumber off the boats, and let it float. Luckily, they were near enough to the island, so the water was only waist deep, so they waded and rescued the lumber, sending each board toward the island, then getting it on shore, piling it on dry land to be rescued at a later date, then getting the boats ashore too, to be emptied of water to row home. Dad said it was really funny to see Professor Sverdrup come crawling on the lumber from his sinking boat to Dad's boat, but when that began to sink also, they both had a good laugh. Later, they finally got the lumber home and the bathhouse was built.

One summer when Sverdrup came to our place, in anticipation of his coming, I painted his boat for him so it was on the water when he came. He thanked me and gave me a dollar bill, the first dollar bill I had ever seen. Silver dollars were in vogue at that time. It was also the first dollar I had earned.

The last summer that Sverdrup came, only he and his youngest daughter Ragna came. It was a real treat for my sisters that Ragna came. My second sister was Ragna too. Ragna Sverdrup was a good musician and had some of her music along. The girls played on the organ and sang a lot while she was there and when they left, she left her music book. This was much appreciated by my sisters and it became their start in learning to play the organ.

It was a joy to have Sverdrup with us. He was an ideal guest, just like one of the family. He was always a perfect gentleman, kind, friendly and always willing to talk, even to us children. Mother was a real disciplinarian, and one time when she corrected us boys for something we had done, Sverdrup jovially said, "I can see, Mrs. Dahle, that you have never been a boy." Evidently, he must have thought that she had been a little too severe with us.

At our evening daily devotions, which we never missed, Dad and Mother and Sverdrup would often discuss and talk about the deeper things of God after the devotions, when we children were gone to bed. Mother was a deep student of the Word, so she enjoyed talking to Sverdrup, to get answers to many things that she didn't understand.

Georg Sverdrup had a love for missions and was the instigator of the Mission in Madagascar. He published a little mission paper called "Gasseren." This little paper told of the progress on the mission field, and in each issue he had a little meditation, always geared to missions. When that paper would come in the mail, my mother would quit whatever she was doing and sit down and devour it, especially the meditation. Practically all of these meditations are printed in *Sverdrup's Skrifer Volume No. VI.*

When the Deaconess Hospital secured property on Lake Minnetonka and built a cabin there, Sverdrup went there and came no more to Farm Island Lake. Georg Sverdrup died in 1907 at the young age of 57. When the news reached my parents, I suppose through the Folkebladet or the Decorah-Posten, they both wept. They had lost a very dear friend, and Augsburg Seminary had suffered an almost irreparable loss. The question on all minds was, "Who can we get to take his place?"

Other Visitors At "Furuly"

Professor Sverdrup must have done a good job of telling his friends about Pastor Ole Dahle's "fisherman's paradise," in the wilderness, south of Aitkin, as we had dozens of guests, Pastors and sometimes also their wives, who spent a week or two with us for several summers. This was approximately between 1895 and 1905.

The accommodations were not the best but who cares about that when you can get good food, have a place to sleep, get a good rest, and catch fish so easily. We did have a roomy house, but the only rooms that were finished, after a fashion, were the downstairs rooms and one room upstairs, which we called the "spare room." None of us ever slept in that room; that was our guest room. That room had a bed and a good mattress. The rest of the upstairs was open except for the girl's room, which was enclosed. We boys slept on "ticks" on the floor. These "ticks" were made of strong mattress cloth, which we refilled every summer with new-mown hay. We used curtains for dividers.

It was during the summer months that we had most of our guests. The first one that I remember, was Missionary Tau, who was home on furlough from Madagascar. He spoke several times in our Cedar Lake Church. He did not stay very long as he was doing deputation work for the Mission Board. Missionary Tau spoke of the need for a teacher at the Girl's School at Manasoa. This enhanced my sister Ragna's desire to become a missionary.

One summer we had Rev. and Mrs. Sveen from Benson, Rev. Gynild from Eagle Lake, Rev. Torvik from Morris, and Rev. Rudi from Sisseton, South Dakota. These four pastors all came at the same time. Naturally Sveen and his wife had the guest room, the rest of them had to take our boy's room and sleep on the "hay ticks" on the floor. We boys moved out to the barn loft.

We had, of course, a pail of water and a wash basin on an apple box and a "slop pail" for the wash water in each room. Some of the men would take a towel along down to the beach, take a morning swim, wash up there in the lake, and dress on the dock. There was absolute privacy as the nearest neighbor was across the lake, about two miles, and no one else was around except the family. For a place to hang up clothes in the sleeping quarters, we had some nails on the wall—clothes hangers were unheard of.

The "outhouse" was on the back side of the house, behind some bushes. In the evenings the wolves would begin their howling and it almost scared the life out of Mrs. Sveen. The howling of the wolves was a bone-chilling sound. They sounded like they were so close by, you would think that they were right outside the door. Mrs. Sveen's husband had to go with her and stand guard with his 22-rifle while she finished her chores!

When these pastors got together, they had so much fun. They were just like schoolboys, the day after school is let out. They had the time of their life, fishing, visiting, and teasing each other, especially Pastor Sveen. He was a large man and slow in his actions, just like a big bear, and Torvik was slender and active like a cat. One day Mother had made fish soup, and it really was tasty. This was one of her specialties. Sveen smacked his lips, held out his dish and said, "Det var god suppe, a giv mig in ske til." (That was good soup, give me one more spoon.) Quick as a flash, the other three pastors threw each their spoons on his dish, and asked, "Skal du ha flere skeer?" (Do you want more spoons?) I could almost write a book on the tricks that they played on each other. Torvik was like a little dog barking at a big bear, Sveen.

One time the Sveens and we children went out picking wild raspberries and of course, Pastor Sveen had his 22-single-barreled rifle along. One place we heard a little brush rabbit make a noise and Mrs. Sveen asked what that noise was and he said, "It is probably a bear." This made her more afraid, and he walked around with his 22 and said, "Om jeg bare kunde faa se han." (If I only could see him.) He would take care of the bear, with his 22-rifle!

I do not know how long they all stayed, but am sure it was at least two weeks, but Mother never complained, even though the biggest burden of the work fell on her.

At another time Rev. and Mrs. Helset came and spent two weeks with us. They were very fine people. We enjoyed having them as guests. He was a very fine, spiritual pastor. It warmed your heart to talk with him. I believe he was serving a church somewhere in North Dakota.

We also had many other visitors from time to time; the names of whom I can no longer remember. When we had our evening devotions our guests were always included. These guests were treated just like members of the family and their visits left a good impression on us children. We saw them when they were relaxed and were having good fun together. We also saw their serious side, when they took part in Scripture reading and prayer during our devotional times.

Chapter 10
More Memories of My Boyhood Days

I had a very happy childhood. As I think about it, my memories tumble one over the other so quickly, that it is hard to get it down on paper. Mother was the heart of our home. Father was away from home so much on his preaching missions. Mother had the full responsibility of the home while he was gone. She was truly a homemaker and did an excellent job. She was always singing as she went about her work. I can remember many of the songs, that she sang from memory. I often catch myself singing those same songs, that I heard her sing, so many times. One such song was:

"Om nogen mig flu sporger vil, om grund til salighed
Og om der here mere til, som man bor have med
For uten Jesu saar og blod, som han paa korset flyte lad.
Jeg svarer med it freidegt mod, min grund er Jesu blod."

The gist of this translated would be:

"If anyone should ask me the foundation for Salvation
and ask if there is more needed to be taken along as a remedy
besides the wounds and blood of Jesus, that flowed on the Cross?

I will answer with cheerful confidence, My foundation is the Blood of Jesus."

Mother told me, that while we were still in Duluth, and when the older children, Anker, Astrid and Ragna were in school, I with a "wanderlust" would go on exploratory trips, sometimes getting several blocks away from home. We had a friendly policeman, who while on his beat, would keep an eye on me and would often pick me up and bring me back home. I was about three years old at this time.

It was quite a relief for Mother, when we moved out to "Furuly" on the west shore of Farm Island Lake. There were many interesting things to explore there, especially the nice sand beach and the water to splash in. I just loved the water. I did not need shoes, and with short pants, it mattered little, if they did get wet. There was no sharp drop off, only a gradual slope from the shoreline and out to waist deep water. There was a good sand bottom.

I do not remember anything about the first two years at Furuly, but Mother told me, that one Easter, which was late in April that year, Dad was to have Easter services in our home church, the weather was nice and warm and Mother had decided, that the whole family would go to Easter service that day. The three oldest, Anker 9, Astrid 8, and Ragna 6 years old would walk, and Mother and us three youngest would ride with Dad in the single-seated buggy, to church.

Mother had made a nice "Count Fauntleroy" suit for me. I was four years old and she had gotten me dressed first, and told me "Now Trygve, don't go down to the lake. Stay up here, so you don't get dirty, while I get Borghild and Viggo ready." "Yes," I sincerely promised and had good intentions, but soon I forgot my promise and went down to the beach. I intended not to go near the water, but there was a log with one end in the water and the other end was on shore. I went out on that log, which was slippery as an eel, and slipped off and got wet. When I got back to the house, Mother had the other two ready, and here I came with my clothes dripping wet. She had no other clothes for me, so she had no alternative, but to put me to bed and hang my clothes in the sun to dry. Dad and Mother and the two little ones went on to church. One of my older sisters, very likely Astrid, had to stay home with me. She said that I laid in bed singing, "Paaske morgen, slukker sorgen." (Easter morrow stills our sorrow). I don't remember this, but Mother told me about it. It was very exasperating for her, but also humorous.

Mother had a sewing machine and was a good seamstress. She would take old suits and dresses that were given to us, rip them apart, wash and press them and make dresses for the girls and suits for us boys. She even took Dad's robe, which he did not use anymore and made suits out of it for us boys. There was a lot of good material in that robe. Dad wore a Prince Albert suit when he was at the pulpit.

I do not recall that we had any serious illnesses. We had the usual colds and childhood diseases. We never went to the doctor. Mother had her home remedies that she used. She gave us good home-cooked meals. We had very few pastries. We had good fresh air, pure water, lots of exercise, sunshine and a good night's sleep. We were poor, but *"The Blessing of the Lord, it maketh rich, and he addeth no sorrow with it"* (Proverbs 10:22).

One time Anker and I were playing. Anker had a very dull hatchet. I stood beside him, watching him chop. I had my hands on the block. Anker said, "Take your hands off the block. I want to chop." I was stubborn and wouldn't do it. Anker chopped and accidentally hit my pointer finger on my left hand. It was cut off at the first joint and left hanging by just a little skin on the underside. Anker got scared and ran under the house. I cried and ran to Mother. Father was not at home, and Mother wanted desperately to get to a doctor. The horse was at a neighbor's place. She wrapped my hand up and put me and the baby buggy in the boat and rowed a mile and a half; then she wheeled me in the baby buggy two miles to where the horse was. They were unable to catch the horse, so we could not get to town to the doctor; instead we made our way home again the same way we had come.

Mother did the best she could. She made a splint, and used clean cloths, wrapped it up, and it healed; so I still have my finger, even though it is crooked and one joint is stiff. I have often thought, that if I had gotten to the doctor, he would very likely have amputated it as it was badly crushed. When I was older, I would have liked to have learned to play the violin, but could not, because of that stiff joint.

We had many cozy winter evenings together as a family. Our wood-burning stove kept the house comfortable. We had a heavy sheep skin robe on the floor behind the stove. This was a favorite spot for us boys. The stovepipe went up through the ceiling into the girl's room and on into the chimney. This brought same heat upstairs, later we also had a stove in the girl's room. When it was extremely cold, we would get ready for bed in the corner behind the stove and then make a dash for upstairs and our beds. We had plenty of quilts, so we didn't get cold.

Every evening, before going to bed, we had family

devotions. One of my special memories was hearing Father sing. One of the songs that he taught us children stands out in my memory. That song was, "Jesus er hyrden for de smaa lammene" (Jesus is the shepherd for the small lambs.) The chorus says, *"Lammene, lammene, lammene mine smaa, Kom Hjem! Kom hjem! Lammene min smaa, faarene Ligessa"* *(My small lambs, come home! come home! also the sheep, come home!)* I still get tears in my eyes when I think of Dad singing that song. He sang it with such meaning and tenderness.

When Father was away, Mother would lead us in devotions. She would give each one of us a Bible or a testament. She would choose passages from the gospels, that were easy to read. Then we would take turns and each one would read a verse or two. Ragna had learned to read before she started school. After we had read a passage from the Bible, we would all take part in prayer. Mother would begin, then we children in order, according to age from the oldest to the youngest, who could only say, "God bless Daddy and bring him safely back home to us." We also prayed for our relatives in Norway, that we had never seen, grandparents, uncles, aunts and cousins. We prayed too for our missionaries and for the little boys and girls all over the world who had not heard about Jesus.

I don't remember where we had been, but Mother and I were on our way home one day. We were walking on the "corduroy," crossing the floating bog. This was the same path that we used when we walked to school. About halfway across, a terrific thunderstorm came up and a bolt of lightning struck the ground about two rods from us, and a ball of fire rolled toward one of the many "sink-holes" along the logs and disappeared into the water. It was scary, but we were not hurt, but it was followed by a pouring rain, so we were all soaked to the skin. Mother was carrying the baby, which I think was Viggo. We had another mile to go to get home. Since that time, I have only seen lightning like that two other times. That surely was God's protection, as we were the highest thing at that place, so it could have easily hit us. There were no trees near us, until we got to solid ground.

About three years later, I was going to Sunday school, and was crossing the same corduroy. About halfway across, in one of those same sink-holes, was our young heifer; completely submerged, all except her nose, and one ear and horn, but she was alive, and was breathing heavily. What should I do? It was a mile back to our house, and we had no telephone, neither did anyone else, and there was no one at home but Mother and two or three preschool youngsters. So I went on to meet the Johnsons, who also walked, no bicycle, or riding horse, but we boys ran to neighbors that had horses, to bring ropes, etc. and they came; several men with ropes and got the rope around her horns, and got her head above the water until we got more help. They were finally able to drag her out up to the corduroy to a place where it was a little more solid. She was too weak to be able to get up and of course could not walk. Someone had come with a horse and a stoneboat. It was impossible to get a horse out there, but the men were able to drag the stoneboat out there and get her upon it. The water was ice cold. They covered her with blankets and brought her some hay, and we had to leave her there. There was no Sunday school or services for the men or us boys that Sunday, but we saved the heifer, who was soon due to have a calf.

This incident reminded me of the words of Jesus in

Luke 14:5, *"Which of you shall have an ass or an ox fallen into a pit, and will not straightway pull him out on the sabbath day?"* We missed Church that day, but we saved that young cow. She lay on that stoneboat for three days before she was able to get up and walk home. She came out of it in good shape, and became one of our best cows.

One morning Dad was going to go over to our neighbor, the Johnsons, who lived across the bay. They were getting ready to move to Duluth, and were taking the train from Aitkin about noon. Mr. Johnson was milking his cows for the last time and didn't want to pour the milk on the ground, so he had offered the milk to Dad. He knew we could use it, as our cow was dry at this time.

The bay had partly frozen over, so we couldn't use the boat. The only way to get there was to walk on the ice that was strong along the shore and follow the ice up the bay to the point, over to Johnsons. That is the way that Dad went, but there was one spot that had just frozen over and it was not very strong. Dad thought it would carry him, otherwise, he would have had to walk another half mile or more, so he decided to risk it.

The ice broke under him, but Dad was a good swimmer and he got over to the edge of the ice, but it broke again and again, until finally he was able to get back up on solid ice. If he had not been a good swimmer, he would have surely drowned. He was fully clothed and it was very cold, so that his clothes froze on him.

I was skating, on my way to school, and I had a feeling that something was wrong with Dad, as I should have met him sooner. Finally I did meet him. He was all ice, including his beard, and he was dog-trotting toward home. When I met him, he said, "I can't stop now,

Trygve, I have to keep running until I get home. You go on to school." I skated over to where he had fallen in, and there were the milk pails, floating in the lake, where the ice had broken.

After Dad got home, Mother had to thaw the clothes off him. He got behind the big heater to get warmed up. After they got his frozen clothes off him, Mother put him to bed and covered him up real good. He didn't even catch a cold. He had kept warm by running. It was only by God's grace that he didn't drown. We all thanked and praised God for his protection and that we still had our dad with us.

One nice warm sunny day, Mother was housecleaning and was airing the bedclothes and mattresses. I was out there playing, and Mother gave me strict orders not to jump on the mattresses. I suppose I was about five years old. What could be more fun, than to jump on mattresses. I wanted to obey Mother, but the temptation got too strong and I started jumping on them. In order to punish me, Mother put me in the cellar, where it was dark. When the flooring had been laid in the kitchen, they had used long nails so the points stuck through. I knew those nails were there in the ceiling of the cellar and I had to have something to do. I was sitting in the potato bin, so I started to throw the potatoes up in the ceiling, to see how many would stick to the nails. After a while Mother heard this thumping in the cellar and wondered what I was doing. She let me come up out of the cellar. I don't think that she thought this had been much of any punishment for me, as I had had such a good time.

As a little boy I used to love to walk along the lakeshore and pick up pretty rocks. There were quite a number of Minnesota agates along the shore. I picked up many of these, some I gave away, but I also still have some in my possession. I have had about half of them polished, and they are beautiful.

Father was a nature lover, and he knew the names of the many different trees that we had. We had many hard maple trees. Dad would take branches of the sumac bush, about an inch in diameter and saw them lengthwise. Then he cleaned out the inside, which was soft, and used these to tap the sap from the maple trees. He bored holes in the maples with an inch bit and inserted these sumac spouts, and hung containers under them to catch the sap. We would empty the containers every morning, carry it home and boil the sap until it got thick. This made an excellent syrup. This had to be done at just the proper time in the spring, when the nights were cold and there is thawing in the daytime, then the sap would flow freely.

When I was about 10 or 12 years old I trapped muskrats and skinned them and stretched the skins on shingles. These pelts I sold for six to eight cents each. This money I used to buy my clothes. I bought most of my own clothes, from money I had earned, from the age of 12 and on.

Pearson, who was a Swede, lived on the 40-acre island, and he raised sheep. He had one old ewe that was toothless, and nearly ready to die. He told us that we could have her if we wanted her. We took her, and nursed her back to health. We named her Daisy, and smothered her with loving care. The first year she had twins. This was the start of our raising sheep. The next year she also had twin lambs. I claimed one lamb and Viggo had one. We named them, and when we would call them, they would come running. We'd pick them up and fondle them. We really had a lot of fun with them.

We boys were responsible for much of the chores around home. I can remember when we would be sawing or splitting wood, and Mother would call us for dinner, we wouldn't lose any time in getting to the house. When we got near the door we could smell her wonderful baked beans and her freshly baked rye bread. Did that ever taste good after having worked hard outside.

One time we bought some hay and Anker and I were hauling it home from across the lake. Anker was driving the team and I was sitting in the hay load. It was about sundown and we saw something strange in the sky. I said, "O Anker, look at that funny star with a long tail on it." About two weeks later, when we got the *Decorah Posten,* we found out that the star we had seen was Halley's Comet. This was in 1910.

One night late in December, about Christmastime, we had a chimney fire. We heard the roar of the fire as it went up the chimney. We had a new neighbor across the lake where the Johnsons used to live. They had seen the fire across the lake and they were afraid our house would burn up. This man sent two of his sons over to see about us. They were shaving when they saw the fire and they came with the lather still on their faces. They came full gallop on horseback. We had been able to get the fire under control by the time they came. We had closed all the drafts and put salt in the flame. We invited them in for a cup of coffee and thanked them for their kindness.

One time during the winter, after school, I went for the mail. This was a mile in the opposite direction from home. As I started homeward again, it was getting dusk and I heard the yelping of a wolf. I realized that he was on my trail. I ran as fast as I could toward home. I jumped the gate and ran to the kitchen door and opened it and fell flat on the floor from exhaustion. Mother asked, "Trygve, what's the matter?" I said, "A wolf was on my trail?" The next morning we went out and looked and we could see his tracks. He had come clear up to the gate, which I had jumped over.

Another time, in the early fall, I was coming home from school. There was a steep hill going down to the corduroy. We always ran down that hill and there was heavy woods on that side of the corduroy. It was starting to get dark and as I came running down the hill, I ran right into a black bear. He said, 'Woof, woof, woof," and ran deeper into the woods. I ran as fast as I could in the other direction on the way home. I don't know who was the most scared, the bear or I. At least I saw no more of the bear.

One of Dad's preaching places was Thor, which is south of Kimberly. There was one family there, I believe their name was Lee. The father and his son were out in the woods, gathering wood for the winter. They worked a little later than they had intended and when they got home the mother asked, "Where is Bjarne?" He was three or four years old. The father said, "Isn't he home?" The mother said, "No, he went out to be with you." He had taken the wrong path and had gotten lost.

It was beginning to get dark and of course they were alarmed. They started looking for him and calling to him, but no answer. They got the neighbors to help them search for him. They also notified a Boy Scout Camp nearby and they helped look for him. He was wearing only a light jacket and the nights were getting cold. It was heavy timber country around Thor. They notified the sheriff, and the whole community was out looking for him.

They had almost despaired of finding him, but on the

third day, he came walking out of the woods. He didn't seem to be harmed, in spite of having spent two nights out in the cold. They asked him, how he had kept warm, and he said that he had slept with a big black cow. There were no black cows around there, so the only conclusion they could come to was that he had slept with a black bear. They knew that there were bears in the woods. Needless to say, there had been much prayer for his safety. His parents were fine Christian people. God had answered their prayers.

When Mother's father in Norway passed away and after the estate had been settled, she received a small amount of money, as an inheritance. We were a large family and very poor and could easily have spent it then and there for clothes and other necessities. Father thought the money should have been used that way, as his income was very limited; but I can remember Mother said, "No, I'm going to buy that 40 acres bordering our homestead on the north." Mother felt that if she used the money for running expenses, she would have nothing to show for her inheritance.

She was able to buy it at a very low price. It seems to me, if I remember correctly, she paid only $2 an acre. There was a lot of good hardwood timber on the 40 acres; red oak, white oak, birch, maple etc., interspersed with white and Norway pine. The 40 also bordered the lake, so it added lakeshore to our land.

We boys cut a lot of timber on Mother's 40. It was here that we cut the logs, that we sold to get money, so that Anker could go to Augsburg. We also cut a lot of cordwood on this land, split it and piled it and let it season, and then hauled it to town the next winter. We sold most of it in Deerwood as that was closer by than Aitkin was. One time I hauled a cord to Deerwood and got paid four silver dollars for it. How rich I felt going home with four silver dollars in my pocket.

When Father left Norway, he brought with him a violin that his father had given him. We called it, Father's inheritance. Father's father had been a "spillerman" in Norway, and as the custom was, he would lead the bridal pair as they walked to the church to get married. The "spillerman" (violinist) went first, followed by the bridal pair, the pastor, the attendants, and then the relatives and friends.

Dad thought a lot of his violin. Once in a while, he would take it out of it's case and play for us. We really enjoyed that. This was the only inheritance, that he had received from his folks at Dalsbygd, Dalsfjorden. One time one of the neighbor boys asked to borrow Dad's violin, as he wanted to learn how to play the violin. Not long after this, their house burned to the ground—there went Dad's inheritance.

Father would always call on one of the laymen to give the opening prayer in his services. I remember him calling on Anton Hanson, John Holum, Peder Johaneson, and especially old man Skoog. Skoog always looked up towards heaven when he prayed, and he always started his prayer with the same three words, and often tears would run down his cheeks. He would say, "Tak og Lov og Pris," that is, "Thanks and honor and praise to God." I got such a blessing out of hearing him pray. He was a very happy and joyful Christian.

We had several good friends in Aitkin. One was shoemaker George Tangvald, where we took our shoes for repair. He was a very fine Christian man. He had one leg about 4 inches shorter than the other, but he built up the shoe on the short leg with a thick cork sole, so the short leg was about the same length as the other.

When my mother's youngest brother, Karelius, came from Norway to find work, he stayed with Tangvald at first until he could get settled. Karelius was a carpenter, and was always kept busy. He built houses and specialized in doing the finishing work. He and Tangvald would ride their bicycles out to our place on Sundays occasionally. Karelius was young and full of pep, he could turn handsprings etc. He was full of fun, so we children really enjoyed Uncle Karelius.

Other friends in Aitkin were the Julum family. They had one boy and several girls about the same age as our family. When we drove to Aitkin to take Dad to the train, or when we came back we would often stop off at Julums for a rest, put the horse in their barn, go in the house and have lunch. They were so very hospitable. They farmed a few miles north of town, but they lived in Aitkin, so the children could have it handy to go to school. These were Christian people, but they were too few to organize a congregation.

Peter Nilsen was a friend of my father. They were schoolmates at Augsburg Seminary, but did not graduate the same year. All of Peter's classmates received and accepted calls to churches and were ordained. For some reason, Peter never received a call and therefore was not ordained. He felt very badly about this. He went back to his home in Duluth, and spent all summer, studying the New Testament, especially the Epistles, and prayed to God for a place to work. He had practically memorized the Epistles, especially Galatians, Ephesians and Colossians.

My father invited him to come and hold a week of meetings in his congregation, Cedar Lake Lutheran Church. Because the church was so far north in the parish and the Caza Schoolhouse, where we went to

A Pioneer Church Family

school, was about the center, it was decided to have the meetings in the schoolhouse. The schoolhouse was full of people and Nilsen preached in such a way that people were under the conviction of sin. I remember one man, that crawled on his hands and knees up to the front where Nilsen was standing and preaching, and there he was prayed for and went back to his seat. There was a woman sitting by the window, to Nilsen's right, who was weeping and sobbing. Nilsen stopped his preaching and went over to where she sat and gave her the absolution. He put his hand on her head, and said, "Paa Gud's Ord og mit hillige embed's vegne, tilsiger jeg dig alle dine synder's naadige forladelse i Faderens of Sennens og den Hillige Aands Navn. Amen." (On the authority of the Word of God and my holy office, I declare unto you the gracious forgiveness of all your sins in the name of the Father and of the Son and of the Holy Spirit, Amen.) The woman stopped her sobbing immediately, and thanked and praised God for the forgiveness of sin. Nilsen went back to the pulpit and continued his sermon.

I was probably only six or seven years old at this time. Nilsen had a full beard, about 4 or 5 inches long. As he spoke, he had the habit of stroking his beard. I would sit there and watch him, and he would always miss part of his beard. I was wishing that he would reach over a couple of inches more with his hand so as to get his whole beard along, when he stroked it.

These meetings in my father's church were Pastor Nilsen's start, in the work of evangelism, which he carried on for the rest of his life. He traveled extensively in the Lutheran Free Church, from Fargo, North Dakota and south, through the Red River and Goose River valleys. In later years, in my own ministry, I have met many people who were saved under Pastor Nilsen's preaching.

In the summertime, many of the young men went out west to get work during the harvest and threshing. Many of my acquaintances went every fall. I was sixteen years old now, so I thought I was a man and I too wanted to go out working and earn some money. Mother had seen in the Folkebladet that there was a man advertising for Christian men to work during threshing. He lived at Finley, North Dakota. I decided to go there, and bought a ticket to Fargo.

At Fargo I bought a ticket to Finley, and the agent checked my suitcase to Finley, but by mistake he had sold me a ticket to Fingal, which was on the Soo Line. After I got on the train, the conductor, when he saw my ticket, said that Fingal was not on the Great Northern but on the Soo Line and I would have to change trains at Valley City. On the train, I met a Norwegian man, who was a carpenter, and he was going to Enderlin, which was also on the Soo Line. He was going to build three houses and since I had done some lathing, I decided to go and work with him as a lather, so I forget about the harvest fields, for the time being.

We got off the train at Enderlin. I was a total stranger. The man I was with had a place to go, but I went to the hotel. I had only 25 cents left of my money, so I gave them that for a bed in the hall. I hadn't had any dinner or supper and didn't have any money for breakfast the next day, but went to work anyway, lathing for this man. We got dinner on the job. We were working for the depot agent building a house and he arranged to get my suitcase back to me, although it took about three weeks.

I had been there only a short while when I got sick. I called up the Lutheran Free Church pastor and he recommended a Norwegian Doctor there in town. He told me that I had acute appendicitis and needed surgery immediately. He took me to the depot, bought our tickets to Fargo, and we went together on the train. After we got to Fargo, he got a taxi and took me to St. Luke's Hospital, where he operated on me at midnight. He said my appendix was ready to burst. It was only by God's grace that it hadn't burst. He not only paid for my ticket to Fargo, but he never charged me for his services. He knew I was the son of a Lutheran pastor. I gave him my father's name, but he never sent a bill.

I woke up the next morning after surgery feeling fine. He had caught it in time. I had been placed in a ward, and there were a couple of patients there that had typhoid fever, so after a couple days I started running a fever, so ended up staying in the hospital about three weeks. I had written home about my operation, and they had written to Anker, who had come to Fargo also, looking for work. He came to see me, and that really cheered me up. He brought a couple of girls along with him. They were the daughters of the pastor in Fargo. Anker went to church where their father was pastor. Anker got a job with a threshing rig. These girls visited me again before I left the hospital, and their father, the pastor, also visited me.

When I was able to leave the hospital, I bought a ticket for home. I had written to tell them what day I was coming, and Viggo met me at the depot in Pitkin. When we got home and I came in the door, there was excitement, "Trygve is home," they said. The little ones, Ernst and Dagny, were so excited. Rolf was churning butter with the barrel churn, and in the midst of all the confusion, the plug came out of the churn and cream and buttermilk came out on the floor.

This is the way the first year of my "working out" ended. After having surgery, the doctor said, no heavy lifting. I had to be careful for a while, although I was cutting cordwood again that fall.

I have many more delightful memories of "Furuly" and can't thank God enough for the wonderful home life I enjoyed. Mother and Dad taught us the way of life. They lived what they believed, and taught us by word and example. They both enjoyed the beauties of nature at "Furuly" and Mother once said, "If this place was any more beautiful than it is, we would have no desire to leave it and go to our heavenly home. How beautiful Heaven must be."

Chapter 11
We Move To Starbuck

In the summer of 1910, my father received a call to Minnewaska Lutheran Church in Starbuck, Minnesota. This came as quite a surprise to Dad. He was now 57 years old and not many older pastors received calls; people wanted younger men. Pastor Andrew Olson was leaving Starbuck to accept another call. He had heard Dad preach at a District Meeting and had visited with him. He felt that Dad would be a good man for the Minnewaska church, and it was on his recommendation that Dad received the call. Pastor Olson had preached in such a way, as to bring his hearers into a living relationship to Jesus Christ. His message was, that we are saved by grace through faith, and that not of ourselves, it is a gift of God, and he felt that Dad would continue in that same spirit. After praying about it, Father accepted the call, and promised to be there inside of a month.

We had lived at our lake home for 15 years, so this was a big change for our family. The three youngest, Rolf, Ernst and Dagny had been born there. I can remember when they were born. Mrs. Anton Hanson was the midwife that attended Mother. Anker, Astrid and Ragna were no longer at home. Anker was in Minneapolis, going to school and working. Astrid and Ragna were both teaching school. There were six of us children, besides Mother and Dad that moved to Starbuck.

Now the question was, how were we to move? We had several cows and a horse. We decided to have a sale, and sell everything that we didn't want to take along. We came to the conclusion that we would ship our furniture and our three best cows in a railroad car. There was a man that went along to take care of the cows. We decided not to ship the horse, but that Viggo and I would drive Prince and the buggy to Starbuck. Borghild and I had gone ahead to Starbuck to start high school, and I came back on the train, so that I could join Viggo, and the two of us would drive Prince to Starbuck.

Mother and Dad and the three youngest children took the train from Deerwood. They had to change trains at Little Falls, as Starbuck was on a branch line from Little Falls to Breckenridge. Father became ill with one of his migraine headaches while they were on the train, so when they got to Little Falls, they went to a doctor and then to a hotel. From time to time Father would get these severe headaches, which generally meant that he would have to go to bed for about three days. It was probably the stress of the moving that brought it on this time.

Viggo and I hitched Prince to the buggy and started out for our long trip to Starbuck. We went through Deerwood and Brainerd and south, we had no map, but we stayed on the roads that followed the railroad, from town to town. When we got to Little Falls, we found the folks in a hotel close to the depot. We visited with them a little while and were on our way again. We crossed the river at Little Falls and followed the branch line of the railroad.

We got to Swanville on a Saturday night, put Prince

in a livery barn, and went to a hotel. Hotels were about a dollar a night. The attendants at the livery barn had been drinking and did not take care of the horses the way they were supposed to. Sunday morning when Viggo and I went to the barn to get Prince, he was not there. The men didn't know where he was, and we hunted all over town, but couldn't find him. Then someone came from out in the country and they said, they had seen a brown horse with his harness on in a cornfield, a couple of miles out of town. We went out there and sure enough, there was Prince, in someone's garden. Poor fellow, he hadn't been fed or watered or tied to the crib in the barn, so he just followed his instinct and helped himself to food where he could find it. We led him back to town, first to the watering trough, where he drank and drank, as he was thirsty, and then we hitched him to the buggy and continued our trip. We went southwest, through Grey Eagle and Sauk Centre and then on west to Villard, Glenwood and Starbuck. I believe the trip took us almost a week.

The parsonage where we lived was on the outskirts of town, so we also had a barn, where we kept our three cows and Prince. I don't remember who helped us unload the railroad car when it came, but it was probably the drayman and some of the church members.

Living in town was a new experience for our family. We now had it much handier to get to school, including high school. I started high school with Borghild as a Freshman, but being 19 years old, I was older than the Seniors, and I didn't like Latin and some of the other subjects, so I did not continue. I was offered a bookkeeping job in a new bank, that was just starting up. Arithmetic had always been my favorite subject, so I liked working with figures. I also waited on customers at the window, which I enjoyed. This gave me an opportunity to get acquainted with the people in town. I worked at the bank for three years. The Lord didn't want me in the banking business. Due to mismanagement, the bank was closed, and I was out of a job.

Father's call was to Minnewaska Church, but he also reached out to other places, so he had several regular preaching places; Barsness, Lowry; Johnson schoolhouse, north of Lowry; and places that he went to occasionally, like Glenwood, Alexandria and Hoffman. Miss Sarah Johnson, from the Johnson schoolhouse became a deaconess and went to Madagascar as a missionary and later married Dr. Dyrness, who was a medical missionary there.

Father had a rich ministry at Starbuck. He did much visitation among the elderly and the sick in the hospital. According to his pastor's handbooks he had a weekly class at the hospital. He had prayer meetings, Ladies Aids, young peoples meetings and "Opbyggelse" meetings on a regular basis. An *Opbyggelse Mete* literally translated would be, a "meeting to build up," as the Scripture says, *"But ye, beloved, building up yourselves on your most holy faith, praying in the Holy Ghost"* (Jude 20). It was a time of fellowship and sharing, around the Word of God. Many of these meetings were held in the homes. Most of the time the confirmation classes met at the parsonage.

In the midst of his busy life Dad also found time occasionally to accept invitations to hold three-day meetings at various places. From time to time, Father would have guest speakers in his churches, missionaries and lay preachers. One lay preacher that he had several times was O. M. Anderson. Anderson's daughter, Mabel, later became the wife of my youngest brother, Ernst.

In Father's handbooks there are many references to "Kredsmete." These were meetings of the district. It was generally, the pastors that would get together, although the meetings were open to all. They met about every three months, for two or three days, and it would be in a different church each time, so the local people had opportunity to attend. They would choose a Bible theme and have one man to lead the study; others would take part as they felt led. They would also have fellowship and prayer times. The host church would provide the meals and lodging for the visitors.

There were several hardships during those years, often due to the weather. Father notes in his books, that there had been a bad dust storm, or a severe snowstorm, so that church services were cancelled. They had no snow-removal equipment, everyone carried his own shovel, the roads were narrow, so they filled up easily. Often they would drive across the fields with their horses and sleighs to escape the snowdrifts. Sometimes the trains couldn't get through for days or even weeks, especially on the branch lines. They were dependent on the trains for transportation and for their mail.

The big influenza epidemic struck in 1918. This caused the closing of the schools and cancellation of public meetings. In Father's books he shows several Sundays, "no service due to influenza." Many people died, sometimes several in one family. Our family was spared; I don't remember that any of us had it, although many in Father's congregations did.

According to Father's books, it would seem, that every August, Father and Mother would take a vacation of two or three weeks, and would spend it at "Furuly" on Farm Island Lake. Even on his vacation, he would always speak in one of the churches, either Deerwood or

Cedar Lake. He would have one open air service at the homestead. He had this advertised in the paper and his friends would come, from here and there. How Father and Mother loved to get back to the homeplace. The members of our family would try to get vacations at the same time, so we could be together. More and more, this became a summer home for all the family.

I liked to ski, and some of the neighbor boys, Viggo and I went to the north end of Starbuck, where there was a big hill; here we made a ski jump about halfway down the hill. We did a lot of skiing here and would jump as much as 50 to 60 feet.

Glenwood had a ski tournament one time, and they invited the national skiers to come. This included nationally known professional skiers namely; Ragnar Omtvedt, Barney Ryley, Lars and Anders Haugen and others. I also entered the contest as an amateur. I climbed that 115-foot tower and skied down and jumped off. My jump was 115 feet and I surprised myself by landing on my feet and stood and skied over to the place where we turned around. I got sixth place in the amateur class. My prize was a Parker fountain pen. I had never jumped from a tower before. This was an exciting day. I was one of the markers that kept track of the length of the jumps for the professionals.

There was a doctor in Starbuck by the name of Christiansen, and he thought that it was quite an accomplishment for a local boy to have a part in a National Ski Tournament. In recognition of this, he paid my expenses to other tournaments. I went with the other skiers to three more tournaments; Fergus Falls, Duluth, and Eveleth. My record jump was 151 feet, which was at the Eveleth tournament. The record there of the professionals was 171 feet and this was jumped by Ragnar

Omtvedt. My last skiing was in St. Paul. There after a jump, I fell and broke my ski and that was the end of my skiing career. I had made my own skis.

My sister, Ragna, from early childhood, had felt a call from God to do missionary work. When missionaries were home on deputation work, Father always invited them to come to our church to speak and to tell of their work. They usually stayed in our home. Some of the missionaries, that we had were Missionaries Tau and Jerslad. Hearing these missionaries speak, strengthened Ragna's interest in missions.

In 1910, she volunteered to the Mission Board to serve in Madagascar. She had graduated from Aitkin High School, in three years, as valedictorian of her class. After high school she attended the State Normal School in Duluth. She taught rural schools, and later took some courses at the University of Minnesota. The church paid for part of her education. She was a good student and had a thirst for knowledge. She was preparing to teach in Manasoa, at the girls school. Ragna had a cheerful disposition and had an optimistic outlook on life.

One year the Annual Conference of our church was held in Willmar, Minnesota, I believe it was in 1915, and most of our family attended. We took the train from Starbuck to Morris, and changed trains for Willmar. I don't remember where everyone stayed, but delegates stayed in homes, and Father and I stayed with Father's friend, Carl Backlund, who was a member of Eagle Lake Lutheran Church. We rode with him to the meetings. The conference was held at the fairgrounds.

Ragna was with us at this conference and we were together as a family. Someone took an informal picture of us, as we were relaxing, by sitting on the grass at the conference grounds. By July of 1916, she was on her way to Madagascar. Her traveling companion was Sister Milla Pederson, who was a deaconess. After arriving in Madagascar, they had to go by boat 60 miles up the river to Manasoa. The boat was manned by native Malagasy Christian men. The trip took several days, and they had to camp out at night along the way. This was a very hard trip. After they got to Manasoa, they could speak English or Norwegian with the other missionaries, like Dr. and Mrs. Dyrnes; this encouraged them and helped them to adjust to the new life. Ragna then went to Tananarive for nine months, to study the French language. After this, she went back to Manasoa, where she taught in the girls school.

After the bank closed, where I had been working in Starbuck, my desire to attend Augsburg increased and I took a job wherever I could get one in order to have money to go to school. I took a short course at the Minneapolis Business College and worked for a while as a bookkeeper in Minneapolis. One winter, I worked on weekends, as a janitor at Elmwood Lutheran Church. I attended the Preparatory School (high school) at Augsburg, parts of two years.

My first car was a 1910 Model-T Ford, which I bought secondhand. It had no doors in front. It had straps on both sides from the top down to the radiator. It had 50,000 miles on it. I called it my "Prohibition Ford," as it had been used by the United Temperance Workers.

One summer, I traveled in this car to Wisconsin, where I sold Bibles, hymn books, and *Sverdrup's Skrifters* (a six volume set of Georg Sverdrups writings), for the LFC Book Concern.

As I was driving towards Wisconsin, just after crossing the Mississippi River, all of a sudden the car wanted to go to the left and I turned the steering wheel toward the right; but the car kept going left, and went off the road, into the ditch and stopped by a barbed wire fence. I got out and investigated, to see what had happened, and I noticed that the cross-bar from the steering wheel had jumped off the ball and socket. I went over to a barbed wire fence and cut a piece of wire off about a foot long and crawled under the car; put the things back in place and wired it together and drove the rest of the summer, with it that way, and had no further difficulty. At the end of the summer I sold my car for $50 to a construction worker.

My second car was a 1914 Model-T Ford touring car, which I bought from Viggo. He bought another car. Viggo had been selling products for the Fergus Falls Woolen Mills and had had good success, especially up in northern Minnesota in a Finnish community. The next summer, I did the same, working out of Starbuck. This proved to be profitable, for me also.

While in Minneapolis, Anker and I roomed together for a time. This was on 11th Avenue, about a block from Augsburg. On Sundays we attended Olivet Lutheran Church. This was the first LFC church in Minneapolis to use the English language in all of its services. My sister, Astrid, was attending the University of Minnesota at this time, and sometimes she would come over to our place and go with us to church.

One Sunday night we went to Olivet Church to hear Leif Awes speak. He had been accepted by the Mission Board to go to Madagascar as a missionary; however, the Mission Board would not send him out unless he was married. After the meeting, Astrid, Anker and I were standing on the Street corner, waiting for the street-car when Leif came out of the church and came over to where we were standing. To my knowledge, Astrid and Leif had not met before and I introduced them to each other. Matrimonial thoughts were the farthest thing from my mind. Leif's father and my father had been classmates at Augsburg Seminary, but our families were not acquainted with each other. A romance quickly developed between Leif and Astrid; Astrid gave up her studies at the University, and wedding plans were made instead. Ragna was already in Madagascar, so this became an incentive for Astrid to accept the challenge to go there also.

March 1, 1917, was the date that was set for the wedding, and how well I remember when Leif and his family came to Starbuck for the wedding. Pastor and Mrs. Elias Aas; daughters, Gyda, Dagny; and one other sister came with Leif. They came to Glenwood on the train at midnight. Viggo and I went with the drayman to meet them at the depot with a team of horses and a bobsled with a double box on it. We had blankets and robes because it was cold, and we had hay in the bottom of the sled.

They were all seated on the bottom of the sled with their backs against one wall of the box. Viggo and I rode the runners. We had not gone very far, when we came to a place in the road, where one sleigh track had been built up because of drifting; it was about a foot higher than the other side, and because they were all seated on the same side, the box over balanced and the sled tipped over. By the grace of God, no one was injured, but everyone slid out into the loose snow in the brush. There were hats, purses, wedding presents, suitcases and much more scattered all over in the snow, and it was midnight. What a mess. We had to help Pastor and Mrs. Aas and the girls. to get on their feet and get up the embankment to the road again. We had to get the sled and box back on the road, fortunately we had a steady team of horses and a good driver. We had to gather up all the things that were scattered in the snow and get them back in the sleigh box and then we were able to be on our way to Starbuck, where Mother and Astrid were waiting for us, with a midnight supper. In spite of the darkness, we found all of our belongings; nothing was lost. This was a never-to-be-forgotten trip.

The wedding was that week, and I was the best man. The day that the wedding pictures were to be taken, I woke up with a bad case of the mumps. Viggo substituted for me, and he got to stand beside the beautiful bridesmaid in my place; how I envied him. Leif and Astrid sailed from New York for Madagascar March 10th.

L to R: Rolf, Ernst, Trygve, Ole Dahle (Dad), Anker, Viggo

Chapter 12
In The U.S. Navy

Jobs were scarce and in the summer of 1918, I was offered a job with a Chautauqua group. I took care of the tent and was platform manager, introducing the speakers and other numbers on the program. I enjoyed this job, it was good experience and it paid well. The programs were of an educational nature and we had many fine speakers, one was the North Pole explorer; another was Per Stromme, a noted pastor and lecturer; we also had a well-known humorist; a ladies sextet and many other musical numbers.

I was responsible for putting up the tent and taking care of it. I slept on a cot in the tent. One night a terrible wind storm came up, which blew the tent down and carried it about a quarter of a mile. I grabbed my clothes and hung onto a little tree so that I didn't get blown away. After the storm subsided, I went to a hotel for the rest of the night. By mistake, the company had sent two tents to that town. Several local people helped me and we were able to get the other tent put up just in time for the first number on the program, which started at 12 o'clock noon.

We traveled to many different towns, staying a few days at each place. I believe we were at Brandon, Minnesota, when my mail caught up to me, including my Draft Notice, which said that I was to meet with the

Draft Board in Minneapolis at 10 o'clock that day and I had gotten my mail at 9 o'clock. As this was impossible, I called them up and told them the circumstances and that I would like a couple days off to say goodbye to my folks and take care of some business affairs. They told me that I could have a week and as the next Chautauqua meeting was in my hometown, Starbuck, I was able to finish up with the Chautauqua, say goodbye to the folks and take care of my business. At the last meeting, the people who were on the program sprang a surprise on me. One of the men made a speech and "bragged" about me and said, "Let's give Dahle a good send off"—and then they passed the hat and gave me what was in it.

I took the train to Minneapolis the next day and reported for duty. They told me that the group I was to have been with had already gone and since those men had already had a week of training they couldn't send me there alone, instead they asked me if I would care to enlist and I said I would. I tried the Air Force, but my teeth were not good enough. I tried the Marines, and I was an inch and a half too short, so they didn't want me; then I tried the Navy, and they accepted me and gave me a date that I was to report for duty.

I found out later that the group I was to have been with, after a very brief training and because they were short of men, were sent directly to the front lines in France and only six of them came back alive. It was only by God's grace that I was not in that group. God had other plans for me. I thank the Lord that I was spared.

I was sworn into the U.S. Navy Reserve, July 2, 1918, and was assigned quarters in the Radisson Hotel. We occupied two floors of the hotel. We marched every day down to our drill grounds by the Dunwoody

Institute for practice and marched back again when practice was over.

I started out in communications, but had difficulty learning the Morse code. I was able to send messages but had problems with the receiving part of it. I transferred to the baking school. Dunwoody Institute had one of the best baking schools in the country. This course lasted about 10–12 weeks. I really enjoyed this and received good grades. My grades on my notebook work were 3.98–4.00.(4.00 was the top grade).

We had a thorough instruction in the art of baking, starting with the basics and on up. We learned all about the different types of flour and the science of how it interacts with the other ingredients. Occident flour was considered the best bread flour on the market at that time according to our tests. All our recipes were by weight. Our large size bread dough was: 276 lbs. wheat flour, 24 lbs. corn flour, 155 lbs. water, 5 lbs. salt, 4 lbs. sugar, 4 lbs. malt, 5 lbs. compressed yeast, 3 lbs. lard. This made 430–440 pound loaves of bread. We also made muffins, pies, cupcakes, cookies, cakes, etc.

We used about 900 loaves of bread a day for our men and we also baked for the Army men, who were stationed in the West Hotel in Minneapolis. The bread for them was delivered daily by an auto truck from our bakery to the West Hotel.

After I graduated from the baking course, because I had the best marks of anyone in my class, I was retained as assistant instructor and received the rating of Baker First Class from the Navy. That rating was comparable to top Sergeant in the Army.

The Armistice was signed November 11, 1918, which lifted several restrictions for us. We were in our barracks, in the Radisson Hotel, when the news broke, but we were not allowed to leave the building. We looked out the windows and could see that the street was full of shouting, joyful people—"Hooray!" the war is over. Seventh Street was filled with people between Nicollet and Hennepin Avenue. There were very few cars in 1918, but if there had been, they couldn't have gotten through on Seventh Street, because of the people.

During the influenza epidemic, many soldiers and sailors lost their lives, including many from our company, but by the grace of God I was spared.

I could have been released from active duty in March of 1919, except for the fact that I had requested sea duty. I told my recruiting officer, "I'm supposed to be a sailor, but I haven't seen the ocean or a ship, so I would like to go to sea." The officer laughed and said, "Okay, we'll send you east to Captain Stone's Navy in Brooklyn, and he will assign you as to where you will go." Immediately they shipped me east.

I was assigned for duty as one of the bakers on the USS Otsego, which formerly was a German Freighter (Prince Itel Fredrick II) interned in the USA and made into a Transport Ship to help bring the victorious Army home. We were to have pulled out of the New York harbor 6:30 a.m. on March 10th, but because of the sudden accidental death of one of the crew we were detained for a few hours, while we waited for a subchaser to come from Bayridge to receive the body. The man who died was a fireman, who was killed by an avalanche of coal that fell on him in the coal bin. He was found dead by the next man on duty. We finally sailed at 11:20 a.m., leaving behind the beautiful skyline of New York, the Brooklyn Bridge and the Statue of Liberty shining in the sunlight.

We were on our way across the ocean toward France.

This was a totally new experience for me. When we walked on the deck there was a continuous feeling of unsteadiness because of the movement of the ship, which was entirely different than walking on solid ground. We landed and docked at Bassends in southern France. There were about ten other transports there, each waiting to take a load of soldiers home. It felt good to step on solid ground again. The trip across took about two weeks.

We were eight bakers on the ship, four on duty at a time. We only had the crew to bake for going over, about 250 men, but coming back we had a full load of servicemen, which numbered about 2,000. We would unload them and go back for another load. We made four trips, crossing the Atlantic Ocean eight times.

On one trip when we docked in New York, one sailor said to me, "Tonight I'm going home." He lived in Hoboken, New Jersey. I remarked, "I wish I could go home." He asked me where I lived and I said Minnesota. He invited me to come home with him. We went on streetcars and buses and finally got to his home. His family was very gracious to me and were happy to have a shipmate of their son as a guest. The first thing they did was to go to the basement and bring up some beer and offered me a glass, but I thanked them and refused as I didn't drink alcoholic beverages; then they were going to have a game of cards and I didn't play cards; next they turned on the phonograph to get some music, rolled back the rug so we could dance, but I didn't dance; so they didn't know what to do with me. Their way of living was different than mine and I was thankful for the Christian home that God had given me. I felt sorry for my friend, as he had not had the bringing up that I had had. I guess, they thought I was a funny sailor.

Viggo was in the Army Air Force and I knew he was in France and he would likely be coming to Bassends soon to embark on a transport for the United States, so I was wondering if it might be possible for me to see him. I went to the Army headquarters and asked where the Aero Squadron that he was with was located and found out that they were about 30 miles from us at St. Andre Decubzak waiting to come to Bassends to be loaded. I asked if there was any truck going up that way and found out that there was. I went to my commanding officer and requested a three-day leave and it was granted. I got on the truck and got off where the squadron was located and got a soldier with a motorcycle that had a sidecar to take me over to where Viggo was.

When we got there I saw him outside playing catch with another soldier. He saw that motorcycle coming toward him with a sailor in it and when that sailor stepped out it was me. We hadn't seen each other for two and a half years and here we met in France. He took me to his barracks, introduced me to his commanding officer, who welcomed me, and asked if he could get a three-day leave so he could go back with me to my ship.

While visiting with Viggo, he told me there were several of our high school friends from Starbuck who were also there waiting to get on boats to go home. He took me to where they were and we had a good visit together.

Viggo was granted his leave and we went back to the ship together. I took him to the bake shop and fed him up on pie—he hadn't seen pie since he left the USA. Needless to say, we had a good time together and we were hoping that his squadron would be assigned to our ship, but that did not happen. They sailed one day ahead of us.

We got together again when we got to New York and had three days together. Among other things we went to Coney Island. We had our pictures taken there. He was discharged and went home and our ship went back to France for another load.

I didn't have much trouble with seasickness, but there were a few times that it bothered me. Sometimes when the ocean was rough and I felt it coming on I would go up on the top deck and fix my eyes on the horizon and walk back and forth and that would relieve me.

Besides being a baker, I was what they called the "dusty," that is, I took care of the supplies in the storeroom. Sometimes the YMCA, Red Cross, or some other organization would issue treats for us, candy bars and such like. They were given to me to distribute to the servicemen. I had easy access to them and since I hadn't had any candy bars for a long time, one time I ate too many, we were just leaving the harbor and hit rough sea, so I had to feed the sharks.

Sometimes when the ship tossed around it was very difficult to get our work done. One time we had made 40 pies and we had to hold each pie while it was being filled, get it in the oven as quickly as possible and shut the door. Taking it out of the oven was also a problem. One person had to hold the oven door, while the other one took the pies out and put them in the cabinet to cool. That day 12 of them slid off the shelf of the cooling cabinet onto the deck and we too slid clear across the deck and back, as the ship rolled.

When we would arrive at New York with a load of troops, one of the things we looked forward to with great anticipation was to get our mail, which had been piling up.

On one of our first trips back, when I got my mail, I had a letter from home and when I opened it the first thing that I read was, "Ragna is dead." Ragna, my sister, was a missionary serving the Lord in Madagascar and she was taken, I was in the service of Uncle Sam in the Navy and I was spared. I wept as I went to the Lord in prayer and was reminded of this verse, *"For my thoughts are not your thoughts, neither are your ways my ways, saith the Lord. For as the heavens are higher than the earth, so are my ways higher than your ways, and my thoughts than your thoughts"* (Isaiah 55:8–9).

Ragna had only served in Madagascar a little over two years, so she was just beginning her work. She died of Black Water Fever. Malaria was common, but people did survive that, very few lived after contracting Black Water Fever.

I had felt the call to the ministry from childhood, but always felt that I was "no good," which was true. I looked at myself and saw nothing, I was a poor student, I didn't like to read or study, I would rather do work with my hands. In spite of all this, God called me. He is not looking for ability, but availability. He can give the ability. *"But God hath chosen the foolish things of the world to confound the wise; and God hath chosen the weak things of the world to confound the things which are mighty; And base things of the world, and things which are despised, hath God chosen, yea, and things which are not, to bring to nought things that are"* (1 Corinthians 1:27–28.)

When I read those three words, "Ragna is dead," it was almost as if I heard God say, "Now Tryg, are you willing to go?" and I answered, "Yes, Lord, I am willing." I told the Lord, "I'll take her place in Madagascar, if you want me to or I'll serve you in the home field, whichever you want. You lead and I'll follow." From then on I made definite plans, that as soon as I was out of service, I would go back to Augsburg and study for the ministry.

On our last trip home we encountered a terrific gale from the northwest. The winds were clocked at 90 miles an hour. Our rudder chain broke and we were helpless; we couldn't steer with the wind and the ship rolled and we almost capsized. Everything that wasn't tied or nailed down fell from one wall to the other. I was "dusty" and was working in the storeroom and everything started to fall off the shelves, so I had to get out of there or I would have been killed. Our food supplies were generally in gallon cans and these all fell and were five feet deep in the storeroom.

The Captain was ready to send out an SOS call for help, but held off while the crew tried to repair the rudder chain. They had to tie the workmen in place so they could work. They finally succeeded and got it repaired and we could steer with the wind and we were saved.

During the storm, many of the sailors, who had mocked me for my Christianity, now came to me and asked for forgiveness and asked to be prayed for. They knew what I believed as they knew that I carried my New Testament in my jacket pocket, where most of them carried their cigarettes. They had seen me as I read my Testament, and often I had tried to talk to some of them about the Lord. Now when they came to me at the height of the storm and asked for prayer, I told them, "I don't have time now, as I'm busy with my work, but if we are still afloat tonight, come to my barracks and we'll have a Bible study." About ten men came and I gave them each a New Testament and we read and studied the book of Romans and had prayer together. We did this every evening for the rest of the trip and they didn't laugh at me anymore; they were thankful to still be alive.

This was our last trip and we all went home. I never saw any of them again. I don't know what happened to them, but I'm sure they never forgot the storm and our prayers together. I hope to meet some of them in heaven.

When I entered the service, I promised the Lord that by his grace, when the war was over, I would come out of the service as clean as when I went in. Life was very different in the service. There were temptations all around.

When we had shore leave, the first thing most of the men looked for was the nearest bar and along with that there were many related temptations. The men felt they were away from home, no one knew them and it wouldn't matter what they did, but I knew that God was living in my heart and it was unthinkable for me to do anything that the Lord wouldn't approve of.

When I went on shore leave, I generally went alone and came back alone. I didn't want to get involved in any of these vices. Sometimes, some of the men wanted to go with me and I said, "Okay, if we pass up the drinking places." They'd probably pass up one or two and then weaken and go in the third place so I would go on my way alone. Many would be drunk when they came back to the ship.

In France it was even worse; there temptation lurked in every doorway. I seldom went ashore, but if I did, there too, I went alone.

I thank and praise God that He kept me through all these experiences.

Chapter 13
My Years at Augsburg

I got out of the Navy early in September of 1919 and went directly to Augsburg and entered the college. I had several offers of good paying jobs; one was with the Zinsmaster Baking Company which was starting a bakery in Duluth and they wanted to hire me as a baker; another one was a bookkeeping job in a business in Willmar; there were other job opportunities also, but to all of them I said, "No, I'm preparing for the ministry, and I don't want to be sidetracked."

During my time in the service, I had been corresponding with a very attractive and talented young lady, whom I liked very much. After I began preparing for the ministry, God showed me, that she was not the one for me, and therefore we parted company. This was a hard decision for me to make, but I saw God's will in it and I was obedient. She did not have the same spiritual interests that I had and would not have made a good helpmate for me.

I spent two years in the college department and took the subjects that would be the most beneficial to my seminary course. Since I had been in the service, and was a little older than the average seminary student, I was allowed to go on into the seminary without completing the college.

My college subjects were all taught in the English

language, but most of the seminary courses were in Norwegian, except Old Testament, which was taught in English by Georg Sverdrup. Some of my other teachers were: E. P. Harbo, Dogmatics; Andreas Helland, New Testament; and L. Lillehei, Church History.

All five of us boys attended Augsburg and some of the years that I was there, there were three of us there at the same time. Anker had completed the seminary, been ordained and was serving a church before I got out of the service. Viggo got out of the service a little before me, so we were in school together. Rolf was also in the college, and Ernst joined us later on.

Rolf and Ernst were not in the service. They had been drafted and were on their way to camp, when the Armistice was signed, but then they were sent home again.

Originally, Augsburg was only a seminary, with a preparatory school, to prepare young men to go into the Seminary, therefore only men attended. After it became a full college, women were admitted. There were six ladies, the first year it was co-educational. Two of them were the Wold sisters, Laura and Minnie, from Abercrombie, North Dakota. I have forgotten the names of the others. This was in 1922.

We had a men's chorus, which was called the Augsburg Glee Club. This was composed of 18 men, and our director was Professor H. N. Hendrickson. I sang in the Glee Club all the years that I was there. Although I was a second tenor, I could sing first tenor, if I had to as I could reach the higher notes. It seems we were always short of first tenors, so that's what I sang most of the time. Viggo, Rolf and Ernst also sang in the Glee Club. Most of the years, there were three of us brothers singing in this group.

We went on a tour every year. One year we went to Michigan, and I especially remember this tour, as we had an interesting experience at L'Anse. In one of the anthems we had a sentence, *"Darkness shall cover the earth, and gross darkness the people."* Just as we were singing this phrase, the lights went out in the auditorium; but we kept on singing and as we sang, *"the light shall shine upon you,"* the lights came on again. This was quite unusual and amusing.

On this same tour, while we were in Wisconsin, we had another amusing experience. We were singing "The Chinese March" and one sentence had this phrase in it, *"Ya, Ya, Ya."* This was sung in a staccato fashion, and while we were singing that phrase, a dog that was in the audience came running down the aisle and put his paws on the stage, panted and wagged his tail. I guess he thought we were calling him. Most of our men couldn't help but laugh, and the director got angry; he thought we were laughing at our own song—he hadn't seen the dog. The dog came up on the stage and we locked him in a room backstage. The next number was a trumpet solo by one of the boys; the dog howled the accompaniment.

We also had a quartet, and sang at various occasions in the local churches. I was first tenor; Joe Melby, second tenor; brother Viggo, first bass; and Art Nash, second bass. We sang for several years, and were much in demand at different churches. We really enjoyed singing together and had much good fellowship.

One of our problems while at school was to have enough money to be able to continue. We took jobs wherever we could get them, working during the school year as well as summers. I also had to borrow money in order to finish. I had many good friends who were willing to trust me, until I could pay them back. I had worked one summer, selling woolen goods, before I went in to the service, and that had paid well, so I tried that again for a couple more summers. During the school year, I did some janitor work on the weekends in the local churches; and at the same time helped out in the Sunday school and occasionally filled the pulpit.

We students operated our own boarding club. I was treasurer for several years and the last year that I was in the Seminary, I was the boarding boss; as such I got my meals without cost. The boarding boss hired the cooks and waitresses, ordered the supplies and planned the menus together with the cooks. I sat at the head table, and saw that everything was done decently and in order. I had no trouble, as all of the men were grown up and knew how to behave.

The year that I was the boarding boss, was the first year that the school was "co-ed." We had our tables set, eight to a table, and we served family style, and generally everyone sat at the same table at every meal. They would choose their table in the fall and keep the same place all year. Four of the women students sat at my table. If anyone wanted to change tables, they had to make arrangements with the boarding boss. After the meals, we cleared the tables and everyone carried their own dishes to the window that led to the kitchen.

A few days before Christmas, the head cook became offended about something, I don't know what it was, and she said to me, "There will be no breakfast tomorrow. I'm resigning." I said to her, "Yes, there'll be breakfast, if I have to make it myself." Her daughter was the assistant cook, so they both left. I took over the kitchen, and did the cooking myself, with the help of some students. I couldn't attend classes, as I had to take care of the kitchen. I cooked for 4 or 5 days and then it was vacation. There were no complaints on the meals and no one suffered any ill effects. During the vacation we were able to hire a new cook, and an assistant and they began work when school started again and everything ran smoothly for the rest of the school year.

One Sunday evening I was at a Luther League meeting in Trinity Lutheran Church at 9th Street and 20th Avenue. During the meeting, a drunk man staggered in; he had seen the light and came in to the church. We were through with our program, and were getting ready to go home, but we couldn't leave him there. He told us that he was from out of town, and was staying with some acquaintances nearby, but he had taken a wrong turn and couldn't find his way back to their house.

Some of my friends and I tried to talk to him about the Lord. He not only had gotten lost on his way to where he was staying, but he was lost spiritually also, and that was our concern. He told us, he was from South Dakota and had been down to St. Paul with a carload of cattle and had sold them and had spent all of the money for boot-leg liquor, which he had shipped home, intending to sell it when he got back. If he would have accepted the Lord, he couldn't have gone through with his plans and sold boot-leg liquor, so there was no way we could help him.

We did pray with him, and then I went with him to the address of his friend, where he was staying. As we walked along and talked, he became angry, and doubled up his fist to hit me, but somehow he couldn't do it. He stopped and looked at me and said, "What is that I see in your face?" I don't know what he saw; unless he saw Jesus in my face, or was it my guardian angel, but he was unable to hit me. We arrived at the address he had given me, and I had to leave him there—poor fellow.

Bishop Stoylen, from Norway, had been invited to speak to the Seminarians, and he was staying at the Curtis Hotel. Professor Sverdrup came to me and said, "Dahle, you have a car, don't you?" I said, 'Yes." Then Sverdrup asked me if I would go down to the hotel and bring him to Augsburg. The man who was supposed to bring him, for some reason or other, wasn't able to come. I told Sverdrup I would gladly do that.

I thought this would be quite an honor to haul the Bishop in my car. I was anticipating having a nice visit with him as we drove along. I went down to the Curtis Hotel, and there he was, pacing back and forth in front of the hotel, waiting for his ride. He had on a stove-pipe hat and a full dress suit, swallow-tail coat and all, and I stopped my car in front of him and asked if he was Bishop Stoylen. He said that he was, and I said that Professor Sverdrup had asked me to come and get him and bring him to Augsburg. He stepped down to the car, and was going to get in the back seat, but he couldn't, as that was full of old tires. For him, to have to ride with the chauffeur was not according to social customs in Norway. I was ignorant of this. He almost went back to the hotel but finally submitted and got in the front seat with me and we started for Augsburg. I tried to start up a conversation with him, but his pride was evidently hurt and he wouldn't answer a word when I spoke to him. I stopped in front of Augsburg and he went in, with not even a backward glance at me or my old car.

I was in the class when he gave his lecture. It was a good lecture, but I didn't get much out of it because of the way he had acted toward me. He was from the State Church and I was just a student. If this would have been Ludvig Hope or Dr. Hallesby, the story would have been different. They would have considered it an opportunity to witness to a student. They had an appreciation for the lay people.

One time I was discouraged and down-hearted spiritually. I was also financially embarrassed; I was nearly broke, having only a five dollar bill in my pocket, and I was needing much more to meet my obligations, and I was wondering where I could get it.

I was walking on Franklin Avenue, getting close to Chicago Avenue, and I walked past a store window and saw a beautiful picture on display there. It was a picture of the risen Jesus and Mary Magdelene on her knees before Him. The Scripture says, *"Jesus saith unto her, Mary. She turned herself, and saith unto him, Rabboni; which is to say, Master. Jesus saith unto her, Touch me not; for I am not yet ascended to my Father: but go to my brethren, and say unto them, I ascend unto my Father, and your Father; and to my God, and your God"* (John 20:16–17).

That picture was just what I needed, spiritually. I needed to hear Jesus call me by name and to know that he cared for me. I went in the store and asked the price. They said $5. I had $5 in my pocket, that was all the money I had. I bought it and took the picture with me to my room and looked at it and wept. I knelt in prayer, praying that God would supply my need. He had supplied my spiritual need and through this picture he also gave me the assurance, that he would supply my temporal needs; which he did in time.

That picture has been in my office throughout my ministry, as a pastor, and has continued to be an inspiration to me many times, even now in my old age. I thank God for the risen Jesus Christ. We are not worshiping a dead Jesus, but a risen Savior. As I am writing this now,

I have spent 60 years in the ministry, and I can honestly say, "Hitherto hath the Lord helped us." He has supplied my every need according to His riches in glory in Christ Jesus; physical, temporal and spiritual, for which I praised Him.

While I was in the city, I tried to take advantage of some cultural events. Most of these were held in the Minneapolis Auditorium. Some of us students volunteered to serve as ushers for the season and by doing this, we didn't need to buy tickets. We heard top musicians, well known vocalists and nationally known lecturers. Some of the musicians we heard were: Jascha Heifetz, internationally known violinist; Amelita Galli-Curci, an Italian soprano; Lily Pons, French-born United States soprano; and many others. It was a real treat to be able to hear these outstanding performers.

One of the lecturers I was privileged to hear was William Jennings Bryan. He was a United States politician and orator. He had served as a Congressman, was nominated on the Democratic ticket for President in 1896, served as Secretary of State under President Wilson, and besides all this he was a Christian. He lectured against evolution. He believed the Bible account of Creation. I heard one of these lectures, which was very good, and a statement that stands out in my mind was this; he said, "Where do the evolutionists begin?—with a nebulous hypothesis—we suppose—Where do we Christians begin? We begin, where the Bible begins, 'In the beginning—God'—"

I never forgot this lecture. We stand on solid ground; we believe the Bible, the Word of God. *"Heaven and earth shall pass away: but my shall not pass away."* (Mark 13:31).

We didn't have many athletic events at Augsburg,

only basketball and gymnastics. I didn't play basketball, but I did participate in gymnastics, to keep physically fit. I was captain of the Gym team, the last three years I was there. There were 11 men on the team; three were Dahles, Viggo, Ernst and myself. We had an exhibition once a year. In 1922, I won first place in Class C in the Northwestern Gym Meet, in which 14 colleges and universities took part. We competed on Parallel Bars, Horizontal Bar, Rings, Side Horse, and Tumbling. I received a grade of 96 points in the all-around competition. I received first in three out of the five events. Parallel Bars was my personal specialty, but I didn't get first in that. I believe I got second in that though.

While I was still a student at Augsburg, Father and Mother moved from Starbuck back to "Furuly", their home on Farm Island Lake near Aitkin. This was in 1921, and Father was now 68 years old. The work was becoming very heavy for him, and besides this, the time had come when it was necessary to use the English language more. This was a real hardship for my father, as he had difficulty expressing himself in English. Cedar Lake Lutheran Church had issued him a call to again serve them, as his strength permitted. Whenever any of us boys, Anker, Viggo or I had opportunity to visit the folks, we would help him out and preach for him in English.

There were only four in my seminary graduating class at Augsburg; Olaf Braseth, Harold Bueide, Trygve Dahle, and Einar Dreyer. A few weeks before graduation, we were given invitations from churches to preach trial sermons. After this we waited to see if we would receive a call. I only went to one place, and that was Waubay, South Dakota.

It was a beautiful March day, when I left from

Minneapolis, on the train. I was wearing only my light top-coat, no gloves, a hat instead of a cap, and no overshoes. When I got off the train at Waubay, Rev. Olson was just getting on the train, and he told me to get back on the train and ride to Halmquist, as I was to speak at Tabor in the morning. When we got off at Halmquist, there was a man with a team and a buggy to meet us. We were to drive out in the country twelve miles to his home. The wind had turned to the northwest and we were heading into the wind. He had no blankets in the buggy, and because I was so lightly dressed, I would have frozen stiff if I hadn't gotten out and walked and ran. I ran ahead a half a mile and waited for them to catch up, then I asked how much further it was and which way to turn and they said, just keep on straight ahead. I ran another mile and waited for them again; there was a crossroad there and they said, "turn right" and that's the way we continued until we got to this man's house.

The place that we stayed was one of the smallest homes in the congregation and they were one of the poorest families; but it was that family's turn to host the pastor and here we came, two people, Pastor Olson and I. We had a delicious supper, and it surely tasted good after that hard trip. They were a very fine family, with several children, and they did the very best that they could for us. We had a good time of fellowship with them before we retired. We had to climb a ladder to get upstairs, where we were to sleep, and the ceiling was so low, I had to stand on my knees to get undressed or sit on the bed. We had plenty of bedding, so we had a good night's rest.

The church was a half mile beyond, up the hill, and that's where we went the next morning. The church was on the highest hill around there, and we could see 11 towns from Tabor church. When we got to the church, it was almost full of people; they were waiting for the pastor and the student, who was to preach a trial sermon. When I was through with my sermon, which was not very long, in walked one of the trustees and his family; and the sermon was over! This man was a habitual latecomer. Pastor Olson felt so badly, that he had missed the sermon, but he asked me if I would sing a solo, so he could at least hear me sing, even though he hadn't gotten to hear me preach. I was happy to sing for them.

There were two churches in the call; Waubay and Tabor. I was to preach in Waubay in the evening. I don't remember how we got to Waubay, but I believe there was a man who had a car that took us, and the road was rough and muddy in places, also a few snowdrifts. There was a good crowd in the evening service at Waubay. I both spoke and sang at this service also.

My classmate Einar Dreyer had been out to Waubay and Tabor for a trial sermon a couple of weeks before I had been there. I was really surprised, when a short time after I got back to Minneapolis, I received a call from that parish. I felt that Dreyer was a better man than I and that he should have had the call. When I talked to him about it he said, "No, you got the call; that's where the Lord wants you." He later got a call to a neighboring parish in the same district.

I accepted the call and made plans to move to Waubay and begin my work there, as soon as I was through school. Shortly before graduation, I was told that I could not graduate with the class, as I had failed in one subject. This was a terrible disappointment to me. I told the Call Committee what had happened and they said, "We'll take you as you are, and you can make up that subject later on." So I told them that I would come. Dr. Burntvedt gave me a license to preach and to perform all the other ministerial acts. I was the only licensed lay-preacher in the LFC. Three years later, I made up that subject and was ordained.

Chapter 14
My First Parish—Waubay and Tabor

In June, I attended the Annual Conference of the LFC, which was held in Minneapolis that year and then immediately I moved to Waubay and took up the work in the Waubay Parish.

I began my work alone and lived in the parsonage at Waubay. The parsonage was right beside the church. My salary was $1,100 that first year. I made my own meals, although I ate most of my dinners at the restaurant. I was usually invited out for Sunday dinners. I was very busy in the two churches, prayer meetings, Ladies Aids, confirmation classes, choir practice and many sick calls.

There was one young man, who had just moved into town, I don't remember where he worked, but he was a single man, the same as I, and we often got to the restaurant for dinner at the same time, and would eat our dinner together. He loved to argue "religion" with me. I was no good at arguing, but I quoted Scripture, which he could not answer. One day he said, "Dahle, you never want to argue, all you want to do is quote Scripture." He didn't like that. He could meet my arguments, but he couldn't meet the Scriptures.

I had no car when I came to Waubay. I had sold the old car that I had in Minneapolis. The Tabor Ladies Aid had a picnic, about a half mile from the church, and they made a list of all the members and passed it around to get donations to give to me to help me get a new car. I don't remember the amount of the gift, but when the Waubay people heard about what the Tabor people had done, they also made a list and gave me a donation.

One of the members of the Waubay church had a Ford dealership in town. The cars came in on a flat-car; new cars were shipped in by rail; and they had to assemble them locally, put on the wheels, etc., before they could sell them. I worked for this dealer, as time permitted, and helped assemble them and get them ready for sale. In one shipment, there was a coupe and this was the car I chose. I helped assemble my own car and I gave every burr an extra tightening to be sure it was okay.

With the money I had gotten, I was able to buy this 1923 Model-T Ford Coupe. It probably cost about $400. The dealer gave me an extra good deal on it. Was I ever proud of my new car. It was the first new car that I had had and I really dolled it up. I put vases by the front windows to put flowers in and later on I put on 4-inch balloon tires; it rode like a baby buggy.

I really enjoyed that Ford Coupe of mine. It was an open winter the first year I was at Waubay. Sometimes, maybe every third week, I would drive to Tabor on Saturday and have confirmation class, stay overnight, preach Norwegian Sunday morning, have dinner at the place where I had stayed overnight, drive back to Waubay in the afternoon and have an English service at night. On my way out to Tabor, I would often leave the road (it was little more than a trail) and take a shortcut across the sloughs and ponds that were frozen over, as they were smoother than the road, and it saved me many miles.

While going to school, I had to borrow money in

order to finish, some from individuals and some from the bank. I began to pay it back as soon as I could, as I didn't want debts unpaid. I wanted to keep my credit good and I didn't want to mar my reputation.

It was common practice for all pastors, who didn't wear a clerical gown to wear a Prince Albert Suit when they were in the pulpit. For several years, I had bought all of my suits from a good friend of mine, M. Klungness, who was an expert tailor and had a shop in Minneapolis. He gave special discounts to theological students. Toward spring, in my Senior year at the seminary, I had him make me a Prince Albert Suit. I ordered it with two pair of trousers, one plain black and the other striped. This was my pulpit suit for the first 25 years of my ministry.

I started a choir in each of the churches and I directed them both. Tabor especially had some very excellent singers, both men and women. We sang both Norwegian and English. We used mostly the "Frydetoner" which had a good selection of spiritual songs and hymns. Our choir was considered one of the best in the community and we had many invitations to sing in other churches and at district meetings, etc.

Most of the services were conducted in the Norwegian language; two Norwegian to one English, in both churches. The Luther League meetings were all in English.

We were always conscientious in visiting the sick and the older people. We sought to bring our confirmands into a personal relationship with the Lord. There was a very receptive spirit in both of the congregations. Prayer meetings were well attended and we enjoyed much good Christian fellowship with one another.

The Waubay Ladies Aid had an auction sale and picnic in the Tastad Grove. John Tastad was one of my best trustees. The auctioneer held up a quilt and said, "This is our last item, but we're not going to sell it, we're going to give it to Pastor Dahle instead." Then he asked for four men to take each their corner and hold up the quilt and he said, anyone who wants to give a donation to the Ladies Aid for the quilt can throw their money into the quilt, whether it is 5 cents or 5 dollars. The money will go to the Ladies Aid for the quilt, but the quilt is a gift to Pastor Dahle. All the members in both churches were very hospitable and kind toward me.

Every year, during the month of August, I took a vacation and spent it with Father and Mother out at "Furuly" on Farm Island Lake. It was wonderful to be able to relax at my childhood home away from the busyness of the parish work. I enjoyed manual labor and it was fun to help my father do some of the things that needed to be done around the place; things that he was unable to do, especially keeping up the road.

I got my axe and shovel and went to work and trimmed the trees and shrubs that hung over the trail that led to our place. I filled in the holes and ruts, and leveled the bumps on the road, so it was smoother to drive on. I also did some fishing, boating and swimming. On Sundays, I often preached English for my father in the worship service or for the Luther League in the evening.

Several of my brothers and sisters arranged to get their vacations in August also so we could be together. We were all busy, each in our place, and hardly ever saw each other during the year except at this time. Anker, Viggo and I were serving in parishes at various places. Ernst and Rolf were in Minneapolis; Ernst in a parish and Rolf as a Doctor of Chiropractic, had his office and practice there. After Astrid and her husband Leif returned from Madagascar, they often spent vacations at "Furuly." Borghild was an R.N. and she worked in many different places, but she tried to spend as much time as possible with Mother and Dad. She had started out as a schoolteacher, but she didn't like teaching, so she took nurses training at Lutheran Deaconess Hospital and became an R.N. Dagny taught school for a few years and after her marriage lived at Pipestone, Minnesota.

After our vacations, we all went back with renewed enthusiasm to our respective places of work, to which God had called us.

In October of 1925, Father and Mother came out to Waubay and visited me. They came out on the train and spent about ten days with me. It was nice to have them with me in my home. I was proud to be able to introduce them to my people.

In January of 1924, I received a letter from my friend Morris Eggen, asking me to come to his parish and have a week of special meetings. I said to myself. "Me?" and I shook my head and wanted to say, "No." Personally I was at a low ebb in my Christian life and I had been contemplating leaving the ministry. Pastor Eggen closed his letter with these words, "Now don't say no, because I know it's God's will that you come." I wept before the Lord and said, "Lord, you know I'm no good, but if you can use me I'm willing to go."

Pastor Eggen was serving at Faith, South Dakota, and I took a train to Mobridge and transferred to the train going to Faith. All the way I wept before the Lord and prayed that I might be a blessing. Pastor Eggen met me at the depot and took me to his home. He lived on a little farm just out of Faith. This was Saturday night. Sunday morning after breakfast, I asked Mrs. Eggen where Morris was and she said he was in the barn doing chores. I went out to the barn, opened the door and there was Pastor Eggen on his knees in the hay, praying to God for this "poor stick" of a speaker that the Lord had sent him. I wasn't slow in finding my place beside him and we prayed and wept together for the meetings and for the people that would be coming.

This was in February, the weather was warm, it was a February thaw, the water was running and the roads were muddy and bad. We had three sessions a day, 10 A.M., 2 in the afternoon and 8 in the evening. Even though the road conditions were poor, the hearts of the people were open to the message and God gave us a revival. People were saved daily at every session. We prayed with people seeking the Lord. People heard and saw me, but God heard and answered Brother Eggen's prayers. About 40 people accepted the Lord that week.

These meetings were mostly house meetings. A man would get up from his chair, walk across the room to his neighbor and ask for forgiveness for something he had done. A husband would find his wife and the two would kneel and pray together for salvation.

I remember especially one man and his wife that rode with us, Pastor Eggen and me. I was sitting in the back seat with them and he was chewing tobacco and spitting and he was under conviction of sin and so was his wife. We let them out of the car at their house.

The next night at the meeting, they told of their experience. They were both under conviction of sin when they came home from the meeting the previous night, but were too proud to tell each other. When the man went out to the barn to do the chores, his wife had knelt in the bedroom and asked God for salvation, but she didn't dare to tell him. When he came in from the barn, with the milk pails; he set the milk pails down and he said to his wife, "Mary, I have surrendered my heart to God." She threw her arms around him and said, "While you were in the barn, I did the same thing, in the bedroom." They both wept together for joy. They rode with us to the meeting and they both told how they had experienced salvation the night before. Many more were saved at the meeting that night also.

At the end of the week, I was making plans to go back to Waubay and Pastor Eggen asked me if I couldn't stay another week. I said, "No, I have my own work and I have to go back home." He said, "If it's the Lord's will, will you stay?" I answered, "Yes, if it's the Lord's will, I will stay, but how can we know if it's His will?" Brother Eggen said, "We'll throw out the fleece, before the Lord." I said, "How do you do that?" And he said, "We're going to a new place tomorrow, and if the Lord gives us souls at that place, will you stay another week?" I said, "okay."

We went out to that place, I think it was Edson, and while I was speaking a man got off his chair and on his knees and prayed to God for salvation. At the afternoon meeting we prayed with two more people. On the way home, Pastor Eggen said, "Are you staying another week?" I said, "I don't know." He said, "You don't know? There were three souls saved today and you don't know?" I wept and prayed and told the Lord and Pastor Eggen I would stay another week.

I sent a telegram to my parish at Waubay and said, "We're having a revival; I will have to stay another week." After this experience, I lost forever the desire to leave the ministry. God proved to me that he could use that which was nothing in his service (see 1 Corinthians 1:26–29).

As I started the work in Waubay, I felt more and

more the need for a helpmate. There were several fine young ladies in the parish, but I prayed God to lead me to the one that he saw would be the best fitted to be my helper. A pastor's wife is a big asset to the pastor's work in his parish. There are so many ways in which a pastor's wife can be a help to the women in the congregation. In these things an unmarried pastor is at a disadvantage and this I realized more and more.

As I thought about this and asked God's guidance, I saw how God seemed to be pointing toward my organist in Waubay. She was highly respected by everyone who knew her, in the church as well as in the community. She was younger than I and had graduated from high school the year that I came there. Along with her graduation, she had received a two year certificate to teach in the elementary grades. She taught those two years in the Tabor community and roomed with one of the parishioners of the Tabor church, so she attended services there. The more I prayed and thought about this, I was convinced that Agnes was God's choice for me. She didn't have a car and so her father would have to take her to her teaching place, and he asked me if she could ride with me as long as I was going to Tabor anyway and I didn't object to that! Sometimes she substituted as organist at Tabor and also sang in the choir.

The time came when I asked her if she would consider being my wife and she answered by saying, "Me, a pastor's wife?" This overwhelmed her, as she thought of the responsibility and of being in the public eye of the congregations at all times. I convinced her that she would do just fine, and would be everything that the Lord wanted her to be. She was a fine Christian girl and I had helped her to come to Assurance of Salvation. I suggested to her that she should take a year at the

Lutheran Bible Institute in Minneapolis, as this would help her to mature in her Christian life. She agreed with me and made plans to do this.

Her father thought this was a very impractical thing for her to do. He thought, now that she was planning to get married, she shouldn't spend the money she had saved from her teaching but rather add to it by teaching another year so she wouldn't be going into marriage penniless. After praying about this, she and I both felt that the spiritual blessings she would receive at LBI would be more beneficial than having the money in her bank account.

She enrolled for that year at LBI. The LBI was only six years old at this time and was still located in St. Paul. She had the advantage of having the original teachers at the LBI, among others, Dr. Samuel Miller and A. B. Anderson.

During the time Agnes was at the Bible School, I rewrote the test in which I had failed while at the seminary. The test was on New Testament exegesis. I wrote the test in my study and had no difficulty, but passed it with a very good grade.

My congregations were very well satisfied with my work and on that basis they requested that I be ordained. Pastor E. E. Gynild who was the President of the Lutheran Free Church at that time came out and visited with me and the people in both congregations, preached on a Sunday morning and went back to his office and gave a good report and approved my ordination, which was accomplished the next year.

Agnes and I were planning to be married at the end of July in 1926, and my ordination date was set for July 11, 1926. When the pastors of the district heard this, they said, "Why don't you get married the same day you are ordained?" This would save them the expense of making two trips. In spite of the inconvenience to us, we agreed to this, and moved our wedding date up two weeks to the same day as my ordination.

Father and Mother came out on the train and Father had a part in my ordination and also officiated at our wedding. The ordainer was Pastor T. O. Burntvedt. He preached on the text for the day during the morning service and following the service the congregation served dinner in the church parlors.

The ordination service was held in the afternoon. Pastor H. M. Hemmingson brought a message before the ordination service. Besides my father and Pastor Hemmingson, other pastors of the district present read Scripture passages and took part in the laying on of hands.

Agnes was the organist and following the ordination service the substitute organist took over. Agnes went over to the parsonage which was on the same lot as the church and changed into her wedding dress. During this interlude Pastor M. Gjerde brought a little meditation and we had arranged with the organist that when Agnes and I appeared in the doorway of the church, she was to begin the wedding march. My father was ready for us at the front of the church; he gave a brief meditation in Norwegian, and performed the marriage ceremony, also in Norwegian, while we knelt at the altar. Agnes Tastad and I were now Pastor and Mrs. Trygve F. Dahle.

Agnes and I took Father and Mother to Morris, Minnesota, that same evening, I believe that my sister Borghild also drove her car to Morris. We all stayed at a hotel that night and the next morning, Father and Mother boarded the train for home and Agnes and I went back to Waubay, where we continued our work in the congregations for another two weeks until August, when our vacation started. Our first plan was to be married the last of July and go directly to "Furuly" for our vacation, but since we changed our wedding date to coincide with my ordination date our wedding trip was delayed.

On Sunday, August 1, we had worship services in both of our churches and also a young people's meeting in the afternoon. On Monday, we began our vacation, as originally planned, and drove to "Furuly" on Farm Island Lake. We spent most of the month of August there, relaxing and visiting with my folks. We also made a trip up to Lake Vermillion for a few days.

After our vacation, we came back to Waubay and continued the work there with renewed energy. Agnes fit into the work very well and took an active part in the Sunday school, as well as the Ladies Aid. She also continued as the organist.

I was the first pastor in the parish, that drove a car to Tabor in the wintertime. It was common practice for those who had cars to put them up on blocks for the winter and then use horses and a sled to get around. I can remember, there were times when I would be out to Tabor and a storm, with a high wind, would come up and partially block the roads. On Monday morning it would be a problem to get back to the highway that led to Waubay. A young farmer, Tvinnereim, would come with his truck and his boys and drive ahead of me. If he got stuck, his boys and I would shovel him out and he would drive on to the next drift and I would follow him in my Ford Coupe. We would continue this way until we reached the highway. There was a lot of snow some winters. I always carried a scoop shovel and shoveled myself out many times. The road to Tabor was difficult in the winter, but I had many willing helpers to open the road. My little Ford Coupe took me through both snow and mud.

In the fall there was a National Luther League Convention at Thief River Falls and we attended it. The pastor's wife from the Wannaska Parish asked us if I could come up there and conduct a week of special meetings. I agreed to come after Christmas, weather permitting. God gave us nice winter weather and we had good meetings. I took a train through Thief River Falls up to Roseau. God gave us a revival, especially in the Salem congregation. There was much joy among the young people. In some instances, whole families came into a living relationship with Jesus Christ. I can remember at least five families, who all came to the Lord—father and mother and teenage children. This was similar to the experience that we had had at Faith, South Dakota, with Pastor Eggen.

Some time after this I received a call to serve the Wannaska Parish. We didn't like to leave Waubay, as the work was going well, but we felt the Lord was calling us to this northern Minnesota parish; therefore we accepted the call.

Our first child, Adelene, was born while we were at Waubay. She was born on a Sunday night at 9 P.M. We had a service at the church that night and I had gotten one of the laymen to take charge. I had a little problem to locate the doctor, but I did find him in town. He was a good doctor and all went well. How proud we were of our firstborn.

We stayed in the Waubay parish two years after we were married. I had been there three years as a single pastor. The people didn't like to have us leave, but we felt this call was from the Lord, and this was the time to make a move. We had a good relationship with Agnes' parents and her younger brothers and sisters so it was difficult to leave them also.

The Lord had blessed our ministry in our first parish, far above our expectations, and we praised and thanked Him for it.

Chapter 15
The Move To Minnesota—Wannaska

Moving into a new parish is never easy; it is hard for the pastor and it is harder for his family, especially when the children are older and have developed friendships in school etc. The move to Wannaska was no exception; we had made many friends in our first parish and now we had to say goodbye to them and start all over again.

When I received the call to Wannaska, I also received a call to the west coast. I had always had a desire to go to the west coast and this was my opportunity. It was a new church, only one congregation, and a brand new parsonage; we would be the first to live in it and the salary was good. The other call had four churches, a poor parsonage, poor roads and the salary was smaller. The people were struggling homesteaders, but their hearts were open to the Word of God.

Personally, I wanted to go west, but I prayed God to guide me, and I told the Lord and the people in northern Minnesota, through their spokesman, Ole Kittleson, if I didn't hear from them by Wednesday, I would accept the call to the west coast. They were in the process of buying the former pastor's house for a parsonage and so the call hinged on this.

I was hoping that I wouldn't hear from them, but very early on Wednesday morning I received a telephone call from Mr. Kittleson, "We've bought the parsonage. Come." My heart went way down into my shoes, as I wanted to go west, but the Lord proved through this that he wanted me in Minnesota. I never regretted obeying the Lord in taking this call. Agnes always backed me up and said, "The call is yours, Tryg, not mine; wherever the Lord calls you, I will go too." Then I called the congregation on the west coast and told them that I had accepted a call to northern Minnesota and therefore couldn't come out there.

Our problem now was, how were we to get our furniture moved? To move by rail, would have been so cumbersome, but again, Mr. Tvinnereim came to the rescue and offered to haul our furniture and all our belongings in his truck. We didn't have a lot of things to move, but yet it filled his truck. Agnes and I and baby Adelene followed the truck in our car. I had traded my Model-T Ford Coupe for a 1928 Chevrolet Coupe.

I still remember, as we drove long, the roads were good; it was in June, the weather was nice, and the farmers were working in the fields. The scenery changed, as we left the prairies of South Dakota and entered into the timber country of northern Minnesota. The fields grew smaller as we left the prairie and got into the woods. As we passed one place we saw a man who was plowing with a horse and a cow hitched together as a team. Tvinnereim had to stop the truck and get out and look at this strange combination. We had never seen anything like that before. It showed how the people had to improvise and make do with what they had.

I had been registered as a pastor, in Day County in South Dakota; now that I had moved to Minnesota, I had to register my certificate of ordination at Roseau, which was the county seat of Roseau County.

My parish consisted of four congregations: Salem, in Malung Township, nine miles northeast of Wannaska; Bethlehem, seven miles south of Wannaska; Bethesda, a mile from Skime, about 25 miles from Wannaska; and Elkwood, at Winner, about 20 miles from home. The four churches involved much driving, and many times the roads were bad, especially in the winter time, sometimes almost impassable. The former pastor had used horses in the winter, but I had no horses, so I drove my car. Sometimes I would leave the road and drive in the fields for a mile or so, to get around the drifts, and then get back on the road. I had to avoid the rocks and stumps, the best I could. There were no graded roads, and, of course, no gravel or black-top. The road to Roseau was graveled.

The first ten miles of the road to Winner was across a big swamp and after that we got into jack-pine timber and sand, where the road wound in and out among the trees. They were Norwegians that lived around Winner; one family had the Post Office and a store.

One Sunday, I was going to Winner, and the roads were such that I couldn't drive my car. I had a good pair of skis, and I got the idea of getting an apple box and I set it up on end on the skis and nailed the bottom of the box to the skis; I borrowed a horse, and fastened the singletree to the skis and hooked on the tugs—so my skis became a sled. I wore a black dog-skin coat, which was light, but very warm; a fur cap and big sheep-skin mittens, which went almost to the elbow; felt boots and overshoes on my feet, so I was comfortable no matter how cold it was.

When I got to the church at Winner, I had a church full of people waiting for me. They had come from here and there where they lived, scattered in the woods. After the service, I went home again the same way that I had come. That was a 40-mile trip; sitting on an apple-box and a pair of skis. After dinner I had a service in Bethlehem and in the evening I was in Bethesda at Skime, so I didn't get home until midnight. I usually had three meetings a Sunday.

I told Agnes never to worry about me, if it got late, as the Lord was watching over me. I was prepared for any kind of weather. I had extra clothes, robes and blankets in the car, so I could spend the night in the car without any difficulty, which didn't happen very often; but I remember one time I got stuck and had to spend the night in the car. In the morning, I walked around the car and saw bear tracks, so I had had company during the night while I slept. I had a tow chain in my car, at all times, so the first man with a team of horses that came by pulled me out, and I was on my way home again.

We had a choir in three of the four churches. We sang the same songs in all of the choirs. I directed them, and I had them sing only well-known hymns, which the people liked the best. When we had Luther League district meetings, I would bring my choirs, and put them all together in one choir, which sometimes would be as many as 50 voices and they sang well. People wondered how I could get a 50 voice choir up there "in the sticks." The reason was, of course, that we sang the same songs, and even though we practiced separately, it was easy to combine them when we got together.

I was raised in the woods, so I felt right at home, in the northwoods. For Agnes, it was different. She had been raised on the prairies, where you could see 30 to 40 miles any direction that you looked, but here the most you could see was a half-mile. Agnes felt so penned in. I was gone at night much of the time to meetings, and she was home alone with the children and when she heard the wolves howl, or the screech owl, with their murderous cry, in the evenings, when it was dark, she was really scared at times, and wished that she was back on the prairie. She was brave and never told me this, until many years afterwards. I never thought of this, as I had heard these noises from childhood, and even though they sounded close by, they were very likely a long ways away, perhaps 2 to 3 miles.

We really enjoyed our work in this parish. In spite of the poor roads, the poverty, and the inconveniences; because of the good reception to the message of the Gospel, it was all so very worthwhile. The people were very friendly and helpful, as far as they were able.

This was during the "Great Depression." Most of the people had very little of this world's goods. One time I was trying to raise a little money for Missions, and one bachelor said, "I have a quarter, I'll give that." That was all the money he had.

One family that I visited had only one chair in the house. It was a badly worn easy chair and grandma sat in it. The rest of the family used apple boxes, wood chunks, or a cream can to sit on.

Winner was in the blueberry country. There was a good crop the first year we were there, and we picked many gallons, bought some, and had many gallons given to us; so that year we canned 165 quarts of blueberry sauce; which we really relished in the wintertime.

Ole Kittleson operated a grocery store and had the Post Office at Skime. He and his wife had a large family. Their house was across the street from the store. One time I was visiting with Mrs. Kittleson and she wept and said, "O, Dahle, I want to do something for the Lord, but I can't, I'm tied down with this big family." I said to her,

"Why Mrs. Kittleson, God has given you a congregation right here in your home. This is your mission field." After I said this, she realized the truth of this; she just hadn't thought of it in this way. She was a fine Christian lady, and thanked the Lord for the opportunity of being a witness in her own home to her own family, as well as in the community.

Three of our children, Trygve Jr., Olaf and Marjorie were born while we lived in Wannaska.

In November of 1932, we moved to Hallock, where we had accepted a call to serve two churches: Two River and Oslo. There were also two preaching places close to the Canadian border.

Chapter 16
Near the Canadian Border—Hallock

The pastor who had been serving this parish was an older man. He was a deep Christian and the content of his messages was very good, but he had a slow delivery and it was difficult for him to express himself in English.

I had been in the Hallock parish at a District meeting and had played my guitar and sang and also preached in English. The people seemed to take a liking to me and soon after this I received a call from them to be their pastor. We felt the Lord was calling us to this parish so we accepted and prepared to move.

This time moving wasn't much of a problem, as we moved in the same district and it was only about 30 miles. We moved in November of 1932. The people of the congregations that we were leaving moved our furniture by truck from Wannaska to Lake Bronson, but they couldn't go any further by truck because of snow blocked roads, so the people from Two River came with two teams and hayracks on sleds and moved our things from Lake Bronson to the parsonage.

The parsonage was in the country eight miles west of Lake Bronson and eight miles southeast of Hallock. It was one mile from the Two River Church. The Oslo congregation was eight miles east of Kennedy and eight miles south of the parsonage. The parsonage was located right by the river, which was called Two River. It was a well constructed house. We had a good well and burned wood for our fuel. There was a garage for the car.

Our parish consisted of two organized congregations, Two River and Oslo. There were many Scandinavian settlers north and east of Hallock. These people had a hunger for the Word of God, so I also had two regular preaching places northeast of Lancaster; one was Juneberry, very close to the Canadian border and the other was Poppleton, which was further south. These were names of communities. Every Sunday afternoon, we had services in one of these two places. At Juneberry, there was an old abandoned church which we sometimes used, but generally we met at the Steien schoolhouse. At Poppleton, we met mostly in homes, H. Eggerud and M. Sveum are two names that come to mind.

We very seldom had an organ or a piano, so I used my guitar to good advantage and we sang and spoke in either language, whichever seemed most suitable for the group. Whenever possible, Agnes and the family would go along and Agnes and I would sing duets. The people were very appreciative and open-hearted to our messages both in song and spoken word.

We were kept very busy as there were many places where our ministry was welcome. When the area was first opened to homesteading there had been people on every quarter section but due to economic conditions and other factors, many of them had left and gone back to where they came from, so now the settlers that were left were very scattered. One place that we went to occasionally was Caribou, which was right on the Canadian border north and east of Hallock. We also had meetings in Lake Bronson and other places.

Sometimes we preached in parishes that were without a pastor and then there were district meetings to attend. The Luther League had three-day district meetings and we always attended and most of the time had a part in the program, speaking and singing. I drove my cars hard and my '28 Chevrolet didn't hold up, I had to replace two axles and one drive shaft in less than a year, so I traded it off for a new 1929 Model-A Ford and I drove it just as hard as the Chevrolet, but I had no trouble. The Model-A Ford was a good car. Later on, I had a 1930 Model-A, and after that I drove V-8s, trading about every two years. I always bought my cars new, thus avoiding large repair bills.

This was during the time of the change over from Norwegian to English. It was a very difficult time for those who didn't know both languages. Some Sundays we preached Norwegian and others English. On Easter and Christmas, we usually spoke in both languages, 20 minutes in each, preaching on the text for the day. In my pastors handbook, I have this notation Christmas 1932.

> Sunday, December 25, Two River: English and Norse—11 A.M.
> Monday, December 26, Oslo: English and Norse—11 A.M.
> Tuesday, December 27, Juneberry: English and Norse—2:30 P.M.
> Wednesday, December 28, Poppleton: English and Norse—3 P.M.

After my Father's retirement, he and Mother spent most of their time at "Furuly," ten miles south of Aitkin, especially summers. The last year Father lived, they spent the winter also at "Furuly." Fathers health had begun to fail and my sister Borghild, who was an R.N., stayed with them.

In January, Father became ill with "old-age pneumonia" and we realized the end was near and that he would not recover. All of us children were at home when the end came. I got there on a Wednesday and he passed away Friday at 5 P.M. January 13, 1933. I had gone to the mailbox to get the mail and he passed away while I was gone.

He had been in a coma for several days and my brother Viggo was standing at the foot of his bed watching him when all of a sudden he opened his eyes wide, which had been closed since we came home, and a beautiful smile came over his face and then his eyes closed again and he was gone. We don't know what he saw, but evidently he was given a glimpse of the place to which he was going or perhaps he saw the face of the Savior, who was welcoming him.

If I had known that he was going to slip away so soon, I would not have gone for the mail when I did. Suffice it to say, we were happy that we had gotten to see him before he went to his permanent home which Jesus had gone to prepare for him (see John 14:1–6). He would have been 80 years old if he had lived until his birthday which was May 15. He had had a very fruitful ministry.

His funeral was in the Cedar Lake Lutheran Church, the church he had founded, and loved, and his body was laid to rest in the adjoining cemetery. Dr. Burntvedt, President of the LFC at that time, officiated at the funeral. The district pastors also attended and brought greetings. My four brothers and I and Luther Vang, a nephew, were the pallbearers.

After the funeral, Mother and my sister Borghild went to Minneapolis and stayed with my sister, Astrid, and her husband, Leif Awes, and the rest of us went back to our places of service. Mother spent her winters with her children and every summer she would spend as much time as possible at "Furuly."

We spent four good and enjoyable years in the Hallock Parish, in spite of snowstorms and blocked roads in the wintertime, and gumbo mud, when the snow melted and when it rained. I carried a snow shovel in the winter and an empty pail in the spring and summer. What was the empty pail for, you may ask? There was no way to get the gumbo-mud off the wheels of the car, except to throw water on them, and there was usually water to be found in the ditches along the road, so I used the pail to dip water out of the ditch and throw it on the wheels and the gumbo would drop off and I could drive again.

One time it took me three hours to go half a mile, but there was lots of water in the ditches, so I made it to the church. The gumbo was sticky and you couldn't use a shovel on it as it would only stick to the shovel, so water was the only thing that would take it off.

Several things stand out in my memory concerning the time that we spent at Hallock, quite a few of these things involved our children and some of them were very frightening.

One evening, during the Christmas season, the Oslo church, some distance south of us, had their Christmas tree Sunday school program and we decided to go, in spite of the 20 below weather, because the roads were open and there was no wind when we left. We got there okay and enjoyed the program very much.

We had the whole family along. It was after midnight

when we started for home, the road was open until we got half a mile from where we lived. A wind had come up from the northwest and it was drifting badly, filling in the tracks of the plowed out road and it was getting deeper as we got toward our house, so we couldn't get any farther.

I took my scoop shovel, which I always carried in the winter, and shoveled the length of the car. Agnes and the children were in the car. I drove the length that I had shoveled out, took my shovel and shoveled another car length, got in the car and drove another length and this is the way I kept on until we got home.

It was four o'clock when we reached our driveway going into the yard. Then I had to carry the sleeping children, one by one into the house; Agnes was holding the bundled up baby. After we all got into the house, we had to fire up the wood stoves as the house was cold. We left the children sleeping in the chairs and on the davenport until the house was sufficiently warm to undress them and put them to bed. This was a very dangerous trip but the Lord was good and we were now home and safe and could go to sleep. After we had the children in bed, Agnes and I knelt and thanked God for bringing us safely home.

Our parsonage was about 100 feet from the river and we warned the boys, Tryg Jr. and Olaf, to be careful and not to fall into the river. One day when I was sitting in my office studying, I heard a yell for HELP. I took the steps down the stairs in about three jumps and ran down to the river and there on the cement slab under the bridge I saw the boys, Olaf in the water and Tryg Jr. standing on the cement slab holding Olaf by one hand, yelling for help. He wasn't strong enough to pull Olaf out, all he could do was to hold onto him and call for help. Olaf was 5 and Tryg Jr. 6 at that time.

I had to climb down the bracing of the bridge to get to Tryg and then I pulled Olaf out. It was the spring of the year and the water in the river was high. His cap was floating down the river and Olaf said, "My cap! my cap!" and I said, "We should worry about the cap, as long as it isn't you, going down the river." Tryg Jr. should have had a medal for saving his brother's life.

One day when Agnes was washing clothes and Olaf, maybe two and a half to three years old, was watching her. He got the idea he was going to help his mother put some clothes in the power-ringer and when her back was turned he got his hand in the ringer and it pulled his arm in up to his shoulder; he yelled and Agnes hit the release button and the ringer opened up so she could get his arm out again. It had gone in far enough, so it had torn the skin under his arm.

I was not at home, but Agnes called a neighbor and they took him to the hospital and the doctor had to take several stitches to draw the skin together where it was torn. God was good.

We bought our milk from our nearest neighbor, but we had to go and get it. One morning I was going to get the milk and Tryg Jr. was going with me, Marjorie, one and a half years old, heard me say this and wanted to go along and unbeknown to me went out of the house and over to the garage and just as I backed out I hit her with the bumper of the car, knocked her down and the hind wheel went over her. I heard a little noise and I said to Tryg, "What was that?" He said, "It is probably Marjorie," and I said, "Is she outside? I thought she was in the house." I got out and there she lay, right in front of the hind wheel.

We rushed her to the hospital and the doctor examined her and said there was nothing wrong with her—she was running around in the hospital. So we went home and the next morning she was cross-eyed. Agnes and I took her at once down to our friend Doctor Skonnord, a good Chiropractor, and he found a couple of vertebrae out of place. She was so small that he couldn't get her on his table, so Agnes held her on her knees and Dr. Skonnord adjusted those vertebrae very carefully and we went back to Hallock and she was alright from then on and never did have any bad effects from that experience.

One spring, because of the mud, I bought Adelene a pair of rubber boots to keep her feet dry. The children had almost a mile to walk to school. The Foss boys and our children walked together that mile. The Foss place was south about a quarter of a mile from our place.

One day, the boys, Tryg Jr. and Olaf, came home but not Adelene. I inquired where Adelene was and they said, "Oh, she's stuck in the mud." I got in my car and drove over that way and sure enough there she stood, stuck in the mud. The boots stuck in the gumbo and if she tried to walk she would only get her feet out of the boots and the boots stood there in the mud. When I bought the boots, I was unaware of the action of the gumbo when it is at a certain consistency. If I had known, I would have bought her overshoes that buckled rather than boots.

When she saw me she started to cry and I never felt more sorry for anyone than I did then. I picked her up and took her over to the car, went back and pulled her boots out of the gumbo and drove home. That experience preached a real sermon to me. There are thousands of poor sinners stuck in the mire of sin and they can in no way free themselves. It takes a power outside of ourselves to do this. Hence Jesus has come to set us free from the mire of sin.

Most parents, like us, have had varied emotionally and upsetting experiences in raising their families; times when they could have so easily lost one of their children by accident or illness. God spared us and while we were no better than other people he saw fit to bring us safely through these times. It is good to have a God to go to and pray to for our protection and God surely was with us and has been with us all through our life—what a comfort. *"Praise ye the Lord. 0 give thanks unto the Lord; for he is good: for his mercy endureth for ever"* (Psalm 106:1).

"Lord Jesus Christ, I flee to Thee, Let me Thy grace obtain! But if Thou shouldest turn from me, My quest would all be vain" (Hymn Number 279 in the Concordia).

The thought in the last line of this hymn is more expressive in the Norwegian, there it says, "If Thou shouldest turn from me, where else, could I go?"

I recall one time when Christmas was arriving, we were not able to meet our obligations. We needed $200 to clear up our debts and we wanted to be able to start the new year with a "clean slate." After the children were all tucked away for the night, Agnes and I knelt in our living room and laid our case before the Lord, and God answered our prayer.

Christmas cards and greetings from friends and relatives came from east and west, north and south and almost every card had a gift in it from one dollar and up. I especially remember one card had a twenty dollar bill in it and that was a lot of money in those days. We received exactly $200, which enabled us to take care of all our indebtedness. How we praised and thanked God.

Our fifth child, Norma, was born while we lived in Hallock. As the time of her birth approached, Agnes had had some false alarms and had been in the hospital, but then had to return home and wait. On this particular day, she was in the hospital again, but since the birth didn't seem imminent, I went out in the woods to see if I could get a deer. It was deer hunting season and we lived in the area where the deer were plentiful. If I could get a deer, this would provide us with many meals of good eating for the winter. I was successful and came home in the evening with my deer. After getting home I found out I had gotten two that day—one deer and the other dear—Norma had been born while I was away.

In the summer of 1935, Our Saviors Lutheran of Grafton, North Dakota, was without a pastor as their pastor, Rev. Hemmingson, had been killed in a tragic auto accident. I was contacted and asked if I could give them Sunday evening services temporarily until they could get a pastor. To this I agreed, as I was the closest LFC pastor to Grafton and I had almost every Sunday evening open. This worked out fine as I had blacktopped road all the way and it was only an hours drive to the Grafton church. Sometimes I was able to arrange to have a morning service for them. This "temporary" arrangement stretched into almost three years when they were able to get Rev. Alfred Knutson as their pastor. I served them about two years from the Hallock parish and almost ten months after moving to McVille. From McVille it was about 25 miles further so it made for a very heavy schedule.

One Sunday, a strong wind came up while I was about half through with the service and I knew that all the roads would be plugged by morning, so I wanted to head for home immediately after the service, but the people wouldn't let me go for fear I would get stranded in some snowdrifts and not get home. I finally yielded and stayed in Grafton that night. As I had feared every road was plugged Monday morning, and North Dakota at that time had very poor snow removal equipment. What should I do? I had work in Minnesota that needed to be done, but how could I get there? I drove around Grafton looking for a way to get out of town but there was none. About noon they began opening the mail routes. I followed the one going north. I knew that there was a new high grade about two miles north that would be passable going straight east into Drayton. If I could get to Drayton, I could cross the river and then would be in Minnesota. There roads would be open and I could get home. But how to get those two miles north was the problem.

The plow from Drayton, which was plowing out the mail routes, turned south instead of north, as the mail route went that way and back to Grafton. While I was sitting in my car wondering what to do, the morning local freight train went north and I knew it would not return until late afternoon, so I decided to take the railroad tracks those two miles. I drove on the ties of the railroad tracks, bump-bump-bump, got to the high grade, drove right into Drayton, crossed the river, and drove home. I knew it was against the law to drive on the railroad tracks, but I was desperate and took the chance. I do not think the Lord will hold it against me. I have no bad conscience about it and I am sure the Lord has forgiven me that sin also. It took me quite a while to live this down, that Pastor Dahle had driven on the railroad tracks.

In this area, driving by car in the wintertime was almost an exception. Most of the people drove horses. I had no horses. A good team of horses cost about $250, so I drove my car as much as possible. I kept my car in good running order and trusting the Lord, I would venture out many times when the weather was bad. The Lord was with me and brought me through on many treacherous roads. One time the roads were bad and the snowplow had not gone through, but somehow, by using my trusty scoop-shovel which I always carried with me in my car, I was able to make it through and some people were talking, perhaps on the party-line and one said, "The road must be open, I saw a car go by." "Oh, no," said the other party, "that's just Pastor Dahle." So that was my reputation—that I could often get through when other's couldn't. Of course, we tried not to be foolhardy and there were times when roads were completely impassable and meetings had to be cancelled and everyone stayed home until things improved.

We have many fond memories of families in the Hallock parish. By God's grace we were able to lead many souls to assurance of salvation and we saw spiritual growth among many of the people.

Chapter 17
Our Ministry in North Dakota—McVille

I had been to some meetings in North Dakota one time and an older Christian layman from the McVille parish was there and heard me speak. I also had played my guitar and sang some of the old familiar hymns. I loved to play the guitar and sing and usually did this along with my messages.

Shortly after returning home from North Dakota, I received a call to serve the McVille parish. After praying about this, Agnes and I felt the Lord was leading us to North Dakota and so we resigned from the Hallock parish in August of 1937, and moved to McVille on November 2, of the same year. The McVille parish was across the Red River, west of Grand Forks, so moving was not a problem as it was not a great distance.

Before moving to McVille, Agnes and I drove to Thief River Falls where we bought a new dark green two door 1937 Ford V-8. It cost about $700. We were able to drive to our new parish in a brand-new car and arrived there at 4 P.M. November 2, 1937. This was shortly before World War II and no new cars could be bought then for several years. Previously I had liked to trade cars often, but as things turned out we drove this car for 16 years and put 227,000 miles on it. We put a new engine in it once.

We moved into a rented house when we arrived in McVille. It was not a very good house, but it was all that was available and the parish did not have a parsonage. Our son, Tryg Jr., who was about eight years old, was ill and had to stay in bed. The roof leaked very badly and one day when it was raining Mrs. Sam Quanbeck came to visit us. When she saw how the roof leaked and saw the utensils we had sitting around in the house to catch the rain, even a kettle on the bed where Tryg Jr. was lying, she almost cried and said, "This is terrible. Something has got to be done about this. We can't have the pastor living in a house like this." She was the Ladies Aid president and so immediately she began talking to the other members of the congregation about the situation.

About this time a very nice three or four bedroom house in town came up for sale. A farmer had built the house for himself but for some reason had to leave it. It was a well-built house. The interior was all finished with hardwood, including the floors. The congregation bought it and we were able to move out of the leaky house into a nice new parsonage. What a blessing this was.

We had three congregations in the McVille parish. They were all rural, New Luther Valley and Zion were out from McVille and Hoff was a few miles from Sharon. Three years later a fourth church was added, East Norway of Aneta. Their pastor had passed away and I was asked if I could serve them. It added very little to the driving as I went past that church on my way to Hoff. This congregation had a Hauge background and they felt right at home in our LFC. In McVille there was a former Presbyterian church which was no longer being used but it was in good condition so we often used it, especially in the wintertime when the roads were impassable in the country. There was a good organ and piano in this church.

We enjoyed our ministry very much in the McVille area. There were many very able laymen who could lead Bible studies and conduct service when necessary, especially in New Luther Valley and East Norway. East Norway was an asset rather than a liability to the total work in the parish.

We kept very busy with Bible studies, worship services, Ladies Aids, confirmation classes and Luther Leagues in all of the churches. We also had a choir in most of the churches. In New Luther Valley we started a string band. We had only a few instruments at first but it grew until at it's peak we had 22 instruments. The band consisted of Spanish guitars, Hawaiian guitars, violins, ukeleles, a tenor guitar and a mandolin. When the string band got up to play there weren't many left in the audience. At first the director, which was myself, had to tune all the instruments. Little by little they each learned to tune their own instruments. This band was really a joy to all who partook and to those who listened. We played familiar hymns that were adaptable to stringed instruments.

Our youngest son, Ronald, was born while we lived at McVille. We had three girls and two boys and Agnes and I had prayed that we could have another boy so we could have a male quartet in the family, Daddy and his three boys. In my pastor's handbook I find this notation about his birthday. "Our boy came today at 5:12 A.M." We now had three boys and three girls. Our family was complete. We now had a full choir with Dad and Mom and the children, two voices on each part. All our children had good voices and sang true to pitch.

These were depression years and the area was also suffering from drought and dust storms. This time was often referred to as the "dirty thirties." Many of the poorer farmers could not pay their taxes and so lost their farms. Money was scarce for all, pastor and parishioners alike. We were all broke.

One of the farmers in the Hoff Congregation decided to sell out and he had an auction. He had a nice Guernsey herd of cattle and we, with our large family, decided we should buy a cow at his sale as there was a barn on the parsonage property where we could keep her and lots of hay was available from farmers who lived along the Sheyenne River. A nice four-year-old cow, coming fresh in two weeks, came up for sale. The owner came over to me and said, "There's a good cow." I bid $50 on her and no one raised my bid even though the auctioneer tried for a long time to get another bid, but he couldn't, so finally he said, "Sold to Rev. Dahle for $50." People told me afterwards "We weren't going to bid against the pastor." The man who hauled her home for me said "I have the mate to her, but I'll not sell her for $50." I said, "How much?" He said, "Sixty-five dollars and she'll be coming fresh in three weeks." I said, "I'll take her." He hauled both cows home for me that day and I went right to the bank and borrowed $115 and paid for the cows. Now we were in the "dairy business."

People started to come and asked to buy milk from us. We said, "We'll sell you milk, but we won't deliver it, you'll have to come and get it," which is what the people did. The people liked our milk because it was so rich, as it was Guernsey milk. We sold enough milk to pay back the loan from the bank and had enough money to buy a refrigerator. I remember how we feasted on all the milk we wanted to drink and ate cream on bread and also made our own butter.

The blacksmith in town bought abandoned cars, dismantled them and sold the useable parts. I bought a front axle with two wheels from him and had him make me a trailer for my car. I bought lumber and built a box for it and also a hayrack so I could do all my own hauling. I hauled my own coal and also hay, which we stored in the hayloft.

We burned lignite coal for fuel. We bought the coal from the lumberyard and when a shipment of good coal came in the lumberman would notify me and I would take my trailer and drive down to the railroad, load my trailer right from the car, haul it to the house and shovel it in the basement. Being I got it right off the railroad car it saved both of us time and money.

We got our hay from the farmers in the parish. Sometimes we bought it, but quite often it was a gift. I would take my trailer with the hayrack on it and drive out to where the hay was and load it right from the haystack, haul it home and pitch it up into the barn to be used throughout the winter.

In the summer, we rented some land for pasture for the cows. It was ten acres and it was close to town. We put an electric fence around it and the cows had great respect for it after one or two encounters with it. We built a feed trough for them and there was also city water available. We drove out there morning and night to feed and milk the cows. We raised one of the heifer calves and so in time we had three cows instead of two.

Our two oldest boys were old enough now to take care of the chores, even the milking, when I was gone. They had their first experience driving the car when they drove out to the pasture to do the milking. It wasn't hard to get them to do the chores when they could drive the car.

When we moved to McVille, a fine Christian grocery man told me I could buy groceries on credit and pay as I was able. I was surprised how quickly that grocery bill grew; the first thing I knew, it was $100. As times grew steadily worse, the grocery man was forced to discontinue issuing credit and went on a cash basis only. I made up my mind that I would do the same, not buy anything unless I could pay cash for it. But this bill I had must be paid. This was a hard time for us.

One day when I came into the store, Mr. Evenson said, "Dahle, come here." I said to myself, "Oh-oh, here it comes." Mr. Evenson said, "I've been thinking about your bill." I said, "So have I, and I'm going to pay that bill as soon as I can." (I had gotten it down to about $30.) He said, "I have decided to do this with it." He then took the bill and tore it to pieces and threw it in the wastebasket and said, "Consider it paid." I had struggled with this bill for a long time and now it was "PAID." I broke down and cried in thankfulness to God.

This experience preached a powerful sermon to me. That is the way God does for us sinners, who are trying our best to pay our debt to God, but are unable. Jesus has come and taken our sin upon Himself, paid for our sin by His death on the cross and marked our bill, "PAID IN FULL." We go free, praise God I am free; my bill is paid. Oh how good God is, accepting us the way we are and cancelling our debt. "Paid by the blood of the Crucified One"—I am saved.

We continued to buy our groceries at Evenson's but only when we had the money, otherwise we did not buy.

One day in the late fall when the merchants were already displaying Christmas toys and gifts, my two older boys and I went down town to do some "window shopping" at the hardware store to see if anything was displayed that I would be able to make. There was no money to buy gifts. The children were all thinking, "Christmas" and wondering what Christmas would bring them. Agnes was busy sewing things for the girls, but what could I make for the boys? That was the question, and that is why we were "window shopping" that day.

In the window of the hardware store, we saw a carom board. It was really two games in one as on the back side there was a checkerboard. The price was more than we could afford but it was something I was sure I could make. I had a piece of one-quarter inch plywood in my workshop which was about the right size. I knew that Agnes could crochet pockets for the corners and also paint the necessary lines on both sides. I studied the construction and approximate measurements of the board and went home and made one out of the piece of plywood that I had. I bought some small staples which I used to fasten the crocheted pockets to the corners. The boys were well pleased with this game, and the whole family had much enjoyment from this homemade carom board. It was used for many years.

Other Christmases I also made toys for the children. I would get my ideas by looking at toys that were for sale in the stores. We would have liked to have bought more things for the children but because of the circumstances we couldn't. The children seemed to understand this and were very cooperative and content with what we could give them.

One day I was downtown and met a friend from another congregation. In the course of our conversation, I looked at my watch and discovered it was nearing dinnertime and I invited him to have dinner with us. I went home and told Agnes that I had invited a man for dinner. Agnes became alarmed and said, "Why Tryg, we don't have anything for dinner for company." She had just been wondering what she could put together for a meal for the family. It hadn't entered my mind when I invited him that we were so low on food. I wasn't aware that our cupboard was so bare. We went into my office and prayed to God about the situation. About ten minutes later, there was a knock on the door and our neighbor, Mrs. Henry Quanbeck stood there and had in her hands a fully cooked meal ready to be set on the table. She had made the meal for her husband and adult son, but for some reason they would not be home for dinner and she thought about the pastor and his family and decided to bring it to them to see if they could use it. God used this means to answer our prayer. We put the meal on the table, our company came, we thanked God and enjoyed the food. In spite of hard times and depression years, we never went hungry. The Lord provided so we never missed a meal.

Agnes was very talented and did crocheting and sewed many craft items. People liked her work and she was able to sell all she was able to make. This gave her extra money which she put to good use.

One summer I also was able to make some extra money to supplement my salary as a pastor. I worked with a carpenter who was building and repairing barns. There had been a severe windstorm and it had damaged or destroyed many barns.

This carpenter had been working away from the area, but after the storm he came home and offered his services to the community to help repair the damages. He advertised in the paper for laborers and I answered his ad. I told him, "I'm not a carpenter but I can be a helper." He hired me and I gave him every day I could spare. He was well satisfied with my work and I worked with him that summer repairing barns and we built two new ones. This added income was a big help. Adelene was now attending Oak Grove High School in Fargo.

The Armistice Day storm in 1940, which took so many lives in Minnesota, (especially hunters who were caught unaware and never got home again) was not as severe in North Dakota. I had been out traveling all that day raising money for Oak Grove High School. I came to a bachelor friend's place about 9 P.M. and he wouldn't let me go on but persuaded me to stay overnight with him. The storm had gotten worse and later we read in the papers concerning the many who had perished in Minnesota.

The next year, following the Armistice Day blizzard in Minnesota on March 15, North Dakota was hit with a devastating, killing blizzard. Seventy-one people lost their lives.

The day started out beautiful, sunny and mild. Many farmers had gone to town shopping that day and while they were on their way returning home the storm hit and many of them never made it, but perished on the way.

I had just come home from a sick call, parked the car and gone into my office and sat down to study when I was roused by the noise of the storm as it hit. It sounded like a big truck in the yard. I went to the kitchen door and when I opened it I realized it was a storm.

The boys were in the barn doing chores. The barn was only about 30 feet from the back door. We had a roomer that always parked his car between the house and the barn. The storm was so bad I couldn't see the car. I put on my Mackinaw and cap to go and get the boys and even though I couldn't see the barn or car, I knew where it was and walked along around the car and headed for the barn which was only ten feet away. I found the barn wall and located the door—luckily the door opened in. The boys were through milking. I took the milk pail with both my hands and the two boys took a hold of my arms, one on each side, and we headed for the car which was parked there and went around it and got to the back door of the house. The wind nearly blew the three of us off the back porch, which had no railing, but we were able to open the door and got inside and were safe.

Seven people in our area perished in this storm. One family of four, two brothers and two sisters, got stuck in the snow and tried to walk to their house which was only a short distance away. They were found the next morning where they had fallen. Two teenagers who had been to confirmation instruction never made it home but were found frozen to death in a ditch huddled together in each others embrace. I was among the search party that found them and it was heartrending.

A deacon from one of my congregations also perished only a few feet from his house. He was found in a little hollow on his knees with his hands in his fur cap. He had lost his mittens, knelt down with his back to the wind and turned up his big fur collar to cover his ears, but to no avail. He was a fine Christian man. I had that funeral and I have never seen so many people, both men and women, weeping and sobbing uncontrollably. It was the hardest funeral I ever conducted.

I continued to have a very busy schedule in the parish. In the same year as the blizzard, Easter Sunday, April 13, I had five services scheduled: Hoff at 9 A.M., Norway at 11 A.M., New Luther Valley at 2 P.M., Zion at 4 P.M. and McVille at 8 P.M. The services at New Luther

Valley and Zion both had to be postponed because of bad roads due to flooding.

This was still the time of transition from the use of the Norwegian language to the English language, so in two of the churches, I used both languages that day for my Easter message. In one of the congregations, one lady became very indignant with me because I had used the English for part of the service. She felt that all of the service should have been in Norwegian for a special occasion like Easter Sunday. An elderly gentleman came to my defense and said, "You, Mary, if you haven't heard enough of the Word of God in these 75 years to get your soul saved it won't help much what you hear from now on. Give the young people the Gospel in a language they can understand." (This conversation, of course, was all in Norwegian.) He was a sensible man.

With the bombing of Pearl Harbor on December 7, 1941, our country was plunged into World War II, both in the Pacific and in Europe. This affected all of our people and every community. Young men were drafted to serve in the armed forces and every day we heard on the news reports on the radio the list of casualties. This naturally affected our churches also. Every church had its service flag showing how many men were serving in the military; some even had the sad experience of having to add a gold star to the flag.

There was an all-out effort on the home front as well. Farmers were busy producing food for the servicemen and the factories stepped up their production of war supplies. Along with this came the rationing of many products. Sugar, coffee, white flour, and meat products were among the rationed items. They could only be bought if you had the ration stamps or tokens. Gasoline was in short supply, so it too was rationed. Pastors, doctors and other essential workers were allowed extra gas stamps. Some of my parishioners that didn't need all their stamps shared them with their pastor, so I always had enough gas to get around to do my work.

At this time there was a humorous cartoon in the paper. It showed a beautiful road with only two cars on it going in opposite directions. As they met they saluted each other. "Hi, Doc." "Hi, Pastor."

This was almost true. There was very little civilian travel. Not only was there a scarcity of gasoline but the cars were becoming old and replacement parts were hard to get, including tires. Tires, if they could be bought, were mostly retreads and they were not very durable.

In 1943, the New Luther Valley Congregation suffered a severe loss. Their church was blown down during a heavy windstorm. The one wall blew down flat, the windows weren't broken, it was as if someone had laid it down on the ground in one piece. The altar was not damaged and there was a lamp without a chimney standing on the altar. It was undamaged and even the mantle on it was not broken.

Now the congregation was faced with a question. Should they rebuild on the same spot or should they buy a church in town which was available at a price of less than half of what it would cost to rebuild in the country. The church in town was a good building and had many furnishings that came with it, including an organ, a piano and a good bell.

This was a hard decision for the congregation. There were strong feelings on both sides. Half of the congregation lived in town and the other half in the country. Some of those living in the country would be retiring and moving to town. It was not easy being the pastor at this time. Finally one of the older leading men who lived in the country and would have preferred to rebuild, but thinking into the future and the younger generation, he said, "Let's buy the church in town and continue the work under the same name." This was finally agreed upon by the congregation and it proved to be a wise decision. Later the Zion congregation, which was only three miles out of town, disbanded and united with the one in town, which made it easier for the pastor, eliminating one service. The congregation continued to grow and prosper.

The years spent in the McVille parish proved to be some of the most fruitful years in my ministry. Because of the unsettled conditions during the depression and the war years, people were very receptive to the ministry of the Word of God. We had many good times at Red Willow Bible Camp and other camps, also at district meetings. We really enjoyed the fellowship of the many Christian families in the area.

We served in McVille for seven and one-half years and then received a call to be the Field Representative of the United Temperance Movement of North Dakota. This would necessitate leaving the parish ministry temporarily and it would involve much traveling. We would also have to move to Fargo as the UTM headquarters was located there. Agnes and I prayed much about this and we finally came to the conclusion that this was God's call for us at this time. We resigned from the McVille parish June 4, 1944, and our resignation became effective September 1.

Chapter 18
Our Move to Fargo

After resigning from McVille, we began to make plans to move to Fargo. Our first concern was getting a place to live as in McVille we had a parsonage but now we needed to provide our own housing. We had no difficulty in finding a suitable house that we were able to purchase and we got immediate possession. We sold our three cows at a little profit and also sold a few other things we didn't need. We moved to Fargo on August 30, and I began my work with the UTM on September 1.

Our house was only a block and a half from Oak Grove High School so this was very convenient for us. The older children were of high school age and all attended there. They could live at home and walk to school. Kenny Eggen, Earl Dryer, David Rokke and another boy roomed with us and also attended Oak Grove.

We joined Pontoppidan Church. Rudolph Larson was pastor at the time. We lived a distance from the church and with my new work, I was away from home most Sundays so Agnes and the family had to walk to church as we had only the one car.

My work with the UTM was very different than the work in the parish. It involved much traveling and my time was spent speaking at high schools and churches.

Our aim was to reach the teenagers of North Dakota through the high schools and to educate the general public on Sundays in the churches in each area.

George Parish was the director of the UTM and he also traveled. He visited the Reformed Churches and I visited the Lutheran Churches of the various synods, except the Missouri Synod who would not cooperate with us. Rev. Parish gave me a compliment one time and said I was the best Field Representative he had ever had.

My weekly schedule began on Sunday when I would speak at two or three churches and present the work of the United Temperance Movement. Then from Monday through Wednesday I would speak in the high schools of the area. Thursday I would drive back to Fargo, spend Friday in the UTM office arranging my next week's schedule and then on Saturday I would drive out to the area I was going to work the following week and so on Sunday would begin a new week again.

My program in the schools lasted about 40 minutes and consisted of two parts. I would show a film and give a brief talk. The film showed the damaging effects of alcohol on the human body. In my little talk I emphasized all the good things the young people had going for them: their youth, good character, good looks, good health, a promising future, etc. Then in contrast I told them how quickly these things could be taken from them if they were to indulge in the use of alcoholic beverages. I encouraged them to say "no" to alcohol.

After my programs quite often young people would thank me for my presentation and many said they had made a decision never to taste alcohol. At several of the high schools I had principals that complimented me on the way I had held the attention of the young people throughout the program.

In our temperance work we made several trips to the state legislature at Bismarck, and we were able to influence some legislation which would make it harder for young people to gain access to alcoholic beverages. One such bill was called the "Divorcement Bill." It made it illegal to sell alcoholic beverages at the same place where food items were sold. No restaurant in North Dakota could sell beer or other alcoholic beverages. The people who sold liquor surely didn't like this.

We still spent our vacation time every summer at "Furuly" on Farm Island south of Aitkin. Mother was still living and spent her summers there as much as possible. It was always good to come home to Mother, after Father had left us. We felt we were one in the spirit and she prayed much for her children and grandchildren that they would all come to the assurance of salvation.

On several occasions, when we would visit her she would say to one of her pastor sons that she had such a longing to partake of Communion. I often had the joy of sharing the elements with her in Communion and fellowship and Borghild or whoever else was with her of the family would take part in the service too.

Mother broke her hip in 1939 but she recovered so she could get around, walking with a cane. Mother was a very deep Christian and an avid Bible student. She continued to be mentally alert and kept abreast of the times.

Mother spent her winters with us children. She visited us for a few weeks at McVille and also when we lived in Fargo. After we moved to Spicer, I used to visit her by taking the train from Spicer to Pipestone. Most of her time she spent with the girls. She was with Dagny and Moselle in Pipestone when she passed away. That was March 10, 1948.

The time I spent with the temperance work was rewarding, but it was also a very strenuous schedule with continuous travel and meetings so after three years I longed to get back into the parish. I told the Lord I would take the first call He would give me.

I received two calls that week. The first one was to Green Lake Lutheran of Spicer. I don't recall who the second one was from, but we kept our promise to the Lord and accepted the first one we got, which was Green Lake at Spicer.

Chapter 19
The Lake Region—Spicer, Minnesota

We moved to Spicer July 30, 1947. With our move to Spicer we were now back in Minnesota. Immediately Agnes and I felt right at home in the Green Lake Congregation. The congregation had begun as a Hauge Synod church, but had now been a part of the Lutheran Free Church for many years. One of the former pastors was Rev. E. E. Gynild who at one time was president of the Lutheran Free Church. I followed Rev. G. A. Almquist.

It was good to be back in the parish ministry again. This was the first time I had only one church. There was plenty to keep us busy. I thought I would have a lot of time on my hands with only one church but that did not prove to be true. Besides the Sunday schedule there were prayer meetings, mission classes with the young people, teenage choir, Ladies Aid, confirmation classes, etc. Agnes also was Sunday school superintendent for a while and she was active in the Ladies Aid.

We enjoyed the lake region and especially Green Lake. The parsonage was on the lake and how we all enjoyed the lake. The children would swim and take the boat out, tip it over, and dive from it. The lake was sand-bottom and we kept the rocks cleared away so we had a good beach. In the fall, when the lake froze over, there was skating until the snow covered it and then later we fished through the ice.

One of my delights, in the summertime, was to take the boat out early in the morning before sunrise and be home again for breakfast and most often I would have my limit of fish. I knew the lake and had certain spots where I knew the fish were. We both trolled and still-fished. We still-fished for pan fish, crappies and sunfish, and trolled for walleyes and northerns. We also sometimes caught Black Bass, both small mouth and large mouth bass.

The parsonage we lived in was a large roomy two-story house. It was right across the street from Orred's store. The house was not insulated, (most houses weren't in those days) so it was a virtual "ice-box." I can remember, in the wintertime, I would dress in the warmest clothes I had to keep warm when I sat in my office studying.

One of my hobbies was doing carpentry work. I asked the Ladies Aid if they would pay for the material if I would remodel the kitchen, making it warmer and more convenient. They agreed to this. There were two old-fashioned high windows which I removed and made them smaller and built cupboards on two walls. After I was done I invited the ladies to examine my work and they said it was just as good as if one of the best carpenters in town had done it.

We made several improvements on the church during the four years I was pastor at Green Lake. The roof had not been braced properly when it was built so it was sagging in the center. As you came driving on the highway and came to the church you could see the dip in the middle of the roof. We had it jacked up, straightened and braced correctly. We enlarged the basement, removed the outside entrance to it, made an inside stairway and a

A Pioneer Church Family

new entry on the south side of the church. We installed a new larger furnace, put flu-wood on the walls and ceiling of the sanctuary and also painted the interior. When REA came through, the congregation voted to rewire the church so we could get our electricity from REA. These improvements helped to make things more enjoyable and convenient.

I was treasurer for the Latin American Lutheran Mission for several years, so I attended their board meetings and also their annual meetings. The annual meetings are held in a different church each year. Myrtle Nordin Huerta was the founder of this mission. We made two trips to Mexico, once in 1949 and again in 1950. We visited the border mission at Laredo, Texas, and the pastors and Christians in several of the congregations in Mexico. One interesting thing we noticed when we were in Mexico, about 4:15 A.M., all the roosters began to crow and later all the donkeys began to bray. If you weren't awake before, you surely woke up when the donkeys started braying. It seemed every family had a rooster and a donkey.

We had a very fine group of young people at Green Lake Church. Our teenage choir, which was a part of the Luther League, brought a lot of blessing to all of us. They had good voices and were so willing to sing. It was a joy to direct them. We sang only familiar hymns, but they sang them well and with enthusiasm. Most of the young people were sincere and lived their lives pleasing to the Lord.

We had good fellowship with other churches in the area, often the Luther League would exchange programs or we pastors would preach in each other's churches. Some of the churches we spoke in were Grace Lutheran in Lake Lillian, Eagle Lake, Nordland, and others. We also took part in the Youth for Christ movement, Bible camps, Luther League conventions and district meetings.

We had evangelistic meetings occasionally with several different Evangelists. Joe Erickson, the father of Rev. Jay Erickson, was our guest evangelist several times. He was very effective and was used by the Lord to strengthen the Christians and to awaken the unsaved.

There were many warm Christians in Green Lake church and we had good fellowship. Sometimes we had "samtale" meetings, maybe on Sunday afternoon or evening. *Samtale* means "sharing with one another". We usually had these meetings in someone's home. The purpose for our coming together was to encourage one another and to do as we read in Jude, verse 20, *"...building up yourselves on your most holy faith...."* We would share our experiences, including our doubts and fears and in this way our faith was strengthened. We concluded our fellowship by praying with one another and for one another.

Even though we were now in West Central Minnesota, we still experienced snowy winters and closed roads. In March of 1951, there were three Sundays we could not have services. I could get to church, as the main road was open, but the parishioners couldn't get there. The side roads were plugged full. The tractors couldn't get through and the snow was too deep for horses. One young man came home on furlough from the army during this time but could not get to his home by car. I took him in my car on the highway to the crossroad. I had both my skis and snowshoes with us. I gave him the skis and I used the snowshoes and we walked to his home from the highway. His parents were so happy he could get home and I was glad I could help him. There were several things pertaining to our family that happened while we lived at Spicer: Marjie graduated from Willmar High School (the three older children had graduated from Oak Grove in Fargo), Adelene was working in Minneapolis, Tryg Jr. and Thelma Finnesgaard were married, Olaf enlisted in the Navy, and Agnes and I celebrated our Silver Wedding.

The congregation hosted an "open house" for us on our anniversary and we had it at the parsonage. They had arranged a program and people came and went in the afternoon and evening. It was a delight for Agnes and me to visit with relatives and friends.

When Canada opened up for homesteading, many people from the states emigrated there and took homesteads. Wherever they settled they started churches. This was true in the Lutheran Free Church also.

In the summer of 1951, I received a call to serve two of these churches in Saskatchewan, Canada; Bethel at Elbow and Skudesness at Lorebum. These two churches had called several pastors who had not accepted and then we got the call. This was the second time we had gotten a call from them. We too hesitated as we liked it in Spicer and we didn't want to go to Canada, but finally we realized this was God's call to us and we told the Lord we would give five years of our ministry to Canada. We were never sorry that we accepted this call as it proved to be some of the best years in the service of our Lord.

Chapter 20
We Move to Canada

Now that the call to Canada had been accepted, we needed to make plans for moving. We inquired about the cost for moving. By rail it would be too costly and also by moving van, so we decided to buy a truck and haul our own.

The parsonage in Canada was smaller than the one in Spicer and our family also was smaller so we had a sale and sold all the surplus furniture and things we didn't need. We moved only the things we would have room for in the new parsonage. The money received from the sale paid for our daughter Norma's year at Oak Grove High School.

I looked around among friends and acquaintances for a suitable truck to haul our furniture in and finally decided on a one-and-a-half ton Ford truck which I bought in Lake Lillian for $350. It had a grain box on it and I built a cattle rack for it. The rack didn't cost us anything, except our work. They were doing some remodeling on the church across the street from us and were discarding some good lumber. I asked what they were going to do with it and they said, "We'll give it to whomever will haul it away." I said, "I'll take it." I went and got my truck and loaded it up. From that lumber I built the rack for the truck. I also built a rack for the trailer which we pulled behind the car.

With both the truck and trailer we had room for our furniture and personal things. I also had 40 apple boxes full of books. The men from the church helped us load and we left October 15,1951. Agnes drove the car with the trailer and I drove the truck. Our son Ronald, then 13 years old, and our dog Peggy changed off riding either with Agnes or me.

We took our time making the trip. We started out on Monday and arrived at Elbow on Saturday. We made several stops along the way: Fergus Falls, McVille (we had a service there), Minot, we visited at Finnesgaards and other places.

We had no difficulty crossing the border, although we did have to pay duty on the truck since I had owned it less than six months. The port of entry officials also wanted the serial number on our refrigerator and sewing machine. They had been loaded first so I would have had to unload the whole truck to get to them. I told them I was to preach in Canada on Sunday and I would be coming back on Monday morning and I would bring them the numbers then and they trusted me and let me pass.

After we got into Canada a little ways we ran into a sleet storm which glazed the roads and slowed us up considerably. I was driving ahead with the truck and I was watching in my rear-view mirror to see that Agnes was coming. Glancing up one time I could no longer see her, so I wondered what had happened. I was able to turn around and go back and I found her with the trailer halfway in the ditch. We were able to unhook the trailer from the car and pull it back on the road with the truck and hook it back on the car and proceed on our way. We saw we couldn't make it to Elbow that night so stopped at a hotel in Milestone overnight. We had to leave both our loads standing on the street overnight, but we prayed God would protect them and he did. We arrived in Elbow at 1:15 P.M. on Saturday and went to Gordon Joel's for dinner and were invited to Hovdestad's for supper. Mrs. Hovdestad was a daughter of the former pastor, Rev. Overlid.

We were made to feel welcome at once and the congregations were happy to again have a pastor. They hadn't had a pastor since the death of Pastor Overlid.

Saturday afternoon we got our things unloaded and placed in the house as best we could and we slept in our new parsonage that night. On Sunday we preached in both of the churches and had dinner at Gustav Tastads. While we were eating dinner we got a call from Spicer that an acquaintance of mine had passed away, the funeral was set for Wednesday and they asked if I would conduct the funeral. This family had no pastor. I said, "I'll be there." My plans were to go back to Spicer anyway, as I had some work to finish there. So I left early Monday, gave the border official the serial numbers they wanted and got to Willmar in time for the funeral. I conducted a Communion service the following Sunday and we also had Luther League that Sunday night and that concluded my work at Green Lake church. I had my trailer with me and had a few things left to haul, including my boxes of books, which we hadn't had room for on our first trip. The years at Green Lake had been good years and we felt we were leaving many loyal friends.

I began my work in the Elbow-Skudesness parish November 1, 1951. The farmers were doing their harvest and I worked for one of the farmers for two weeks. I used my truck and hauled grain for him. After the harvest I sold him the truck for a little more than I had paid for it. He got a good truck cheap, cheaper than he could buy it in Canada, and we got practically a free moving trip from Spicer to Elbow, Saskatchewan. We thanked God for His goodness to us.

Because of lack of pastors, the work of the LFC in Canada was at a low ebb. There was much work to be done to build it up again so we entered into the work with enthusiasm. Many of the churches were being served by fine young Christian laymen, but they had neglected to instruct the people of their responsibility beyond the local congregation, so the offerings for schools and missions was practically nil.

I was elected president of the Canada District and I had the opportunity to visit all the churches. I was able to inform the people concerning our schools and our mission fields. We also had some missionaries come and speak in our churches—Lenorah Erickson was one. When people know of the needs and the blessing that can be theirs through good stewardship they will respond. This was true of our people in Canada as well. It wasn't that they weren't interested, but because of lack of knowledge the work had suffered. As time went on the offerings steadily increased and the people experienced joy in their giving.

In both of our churches, Bethel and Skudesness, we had a full program. The people were warm hearted and very receptive to the ministry of the Word of God. We had a nucleus of Christians in both congregations so we had good Bible studies and prayer meetings. We had a very active Ladies Mission Society and a junior mission band for the school age children.

Music was an important part of the church life. There was much musical talent in both churches so we never lacked for special music. We had a male chorus, ladies chorus, soloists and duets and also choir.

Besides our two churches we had several preaching places where we were trying to revive the work that had at one time flourished. In each place there was a small group of Christians. We held services on Sunday afternoons at these places. Some of them were: Demaine, Prairie College (I don't know why it was called this, but it was a community and we used a schoolhouse there), Beaver Flat, Harley School, and there were other places too. The only services these people had were what we could give them on Sunday afternoons driving out from Elbow. These people were very good about coming out whenever we had a service, but they were too few in each place to form a congregation.

Several of our laymen were gifted in speaking, and because we had so many preaching places, they would help me by conducting services at some of these places. In this way, they could get services more often than if I had to do it alone. Some of these laymen were "Curly" Ganes, Joel Olson, Joe Hovdestad, Gordon Joel, Kaspar Knutson, and others. Dr. Burntvedt, who was President of the LFC at one time, said that Kaspar Knutson was the best layman in the LFC. He, however, preached only in the Norwegian language.

Our Canada District of the LFC had a good Bible Camp at Elbow. It was by the river and was a good campground. A fine Christian man gave me some lumber and I built a little cabin with the understanding that as long as I was in Canada it would be mine but when I would go back to the states it would go back to the one who gave me the lumber. I can remember our little dog, Peggy, she would go along to camp and she would lay in front of our cabin while we were in the meeting.

I think back with joy to those camp days. Many souls were brought to the Lord at that camp. One year we had

Rev. J. O. Gisselquist as a speaker and he was truly a "man of God."

After the dam was built, our camp was flooded including our little cabin. The water was 200 feet deep where our camp had been. The government gave us land on higher ground to relocate our camp, but our buildings were gone.

Our 1937 Ford V-8 had lasted all these years, but it finally had gone it's last mile one day on the way from Elbow to a schoolhouse on a Sunday afternoon where we were to have a meeting. I borrowed some money from a friend and bought a 1949 Ford. Later both of the congregations gave us a special offering so we got the car paid for.

Our family began to grow when our children found their mates. Two of our girls were married while we lived in Canada. Marjorie married Gene Zugschwert and they were married in St. Paul, Minnesota. Norma married Ed Knutson, who was a son of Kaspar Knutson. They were married in our Bethel Church in Elbow and I officiated at their wedding.

I always enjoyed my confirmation classes and one of the highlights of my ministry in Canada was a class of 11 girls that I had in the Skudesness church. They were very good students and they vied with one another to see who could have their lessons learned the best. When we went to have our pictures taken the photographer said, "Where are the boys?" I said, "The boys will come later." That proved to be true. Most of them married and in later years many of them became the leading families in Skudesness church.

In the summer of 1956, we received a call from the Home Mission Board of the LFC to work in the LaPorte, Minnesota, parish. Even though we had enjoyed the work in Canada, we felt now that since we were nearing retirement age the time had come that we should move back to the states and so we accepted the call to LaPorte, Minnesota.

Chapter 21
We Return to Minnesota—LaPorte

It was never easy when we moved to a new location. It seemed we always left part of ourselves in the place where we had labored. This was especially true when we left Canada to take up work in the states again. We had many dear friends in the Elbow parish.

In September, I was asked to speak at the 75th anniversary of a church in Grafton, North Dakota that I had served at one time. I took advantage of the opportunity to do part of our moving at the same time. I took the trailer full of books and other things and hauled them to the parsonage in LaPorte. I had sold quite a few sets of books from my library to students who were attending seminary in Saskatoon. The seminary students liked to buy good conservative evangelical books from pastors who were retiring as some of these books were hard to get in Canada. Even though I had sold quite a number of my books when it came to moving, I still had a lot left.

We had our farewell service at Bethel, Sunday, October 28, but the service at Skudesness had to be postponed until Wednesday evening, October 31, due to an unusually heavy, early snowstorm so the roads became blocked in the country. Both of our congregations gave us farewell gifts, so this helped us with the expense of moving and getting situated in a new place.

Our plans were to leave Elbow for LaPorte about

noon on Monday, November 5, but by the time we got the car and trailer loaded it was nearly 5 o'clock. The car was packed to the ceiling, both front and back seats. There was only room for Agnes and I to sit. In our trailer we had our piano, refrigerator and many other things—really a heavy load. Ronald was not with us on this move as he was at Oak Grove High School in Fargo and our friend, Peggy, our house dog was no more. She had died while we were in Canada. Agnes and I were alone on our trip back to the States.

After leaving Elbow, we ran into heavy fog and had to stop at Keeler, Saskatchewan overnight. We were up early the next day and left at 6 A.M. eating breakfast at Moose Jaw. When we got to Weyburn it started snowing and before we got to Estevan it had turned into a blizzard. We crossed the border at 4 P.M. and by the time we got to Flaxton, North Dakota it was really bad. When we were five miles north of Bowbells we got stuck. We were following a big truck but when he got stuck, due to our heavy load, we couldn't get started again and pass him, so we had to sit there. If he hadn't been ahead of us so we could have kept moving, we would have been able to have gotten to Bowbells, which was our plan.

There was another car stuck ahead of the truck. There was a man alone in that car and he came walking over to our car. I could smell liquor on his breath. He was dressed very lightly; bareheaded and was wearing only a lightweight topcoat. He said he was going to walk and get help at a farm place which he had just passed about a half mile behind us. We could not see the place due to the storm. I said to him, "If you want to live, get back in your car and wait for help to come to us." I loaned him a cap and a heavier coat and he took my advice and got back in his car.

Agnes and I were prepared to spend the night in the car. Fortunately it was not extremely cold and we were dressed warmly. A motorist passed us and when he got to Bowbells he reported that there were some cars stranded on the road and there was a lady in one of the cars.

The sheriff, who lived in Bowbells organized a posse to go out and rescue stranded motorists and they got to us about 10:30 or 11 P.M.. We left our cars and rode in to Bowbells, getting there about 2 A.M. All the lodging places were filled, the only place left was the jail and I didn't like the idea of taking my wife to jail!

We called our friends, Orlin and Evelyn Quanbeck, who lived on a high road about two miles out of town. They hadn't gone to bed as it was election night and they were listening to the returns. (It was the year that Dwight D. Eisenhower was elected to his second term as President.) Orlin offered to come in to town and get us as their road wasn't drifted. We got to Quanbeck's about 3 A.M. and Evelyn had a meal ready and waiting for us. We ate our meal and stayed with them that night. No meal had ever tasted so good before or a bed more welcome. "A friend in need is a friend indeed" was surely true for us that night. It was just like coming home to get to Quanbeck's. We thanked God for his provision for us.

Since we didn't get to bed until the early morning hours we slept late, almost until noon that day. After another good meal, Orlin took me in his pickup and we went and got our car and trailer. We filled our car with gas at Quanbeck's and then Agnes and I continued on our way to LaPorte, Minnesota. This was a moving trip we never forgot.

People from the church were there to help us unload

our car and trailer when we arrived. The parsonage was a large two-story house so we had plenty of room. None of the children were living at home now but they all visited us while we lived at LaPorte.

We served two churches: Trinity at LaPorte and Malvik, a rural church, south of Bemidji. A couple years later I was asked to serve the Aardahl church, which was not far from the Malvik church. We also preached occasionally in other places where there were vacancies. I was always happy to be able to share the Word of God wherever there was an opening. God has his children scattered in many places and we found this to be true in the LaPorte parish as well. There were many believers in this area.

Wherever we lived we always had a good garden of vegetables and flowers, including a large assortment of gladiolus. People often would drive out of their way to view our flowers, especially our array of colorful glads, which were my specialty. We had bought an extra good strain of bulbs from a bulb company and they multiplied each year. We shared our glads with our friends for special occasions like weddings and anniversaries. We also kept the church supplied with flowers on Sunday mornings.

One lady was admiring our flowers one day and she remarked that she didn't have any success with flowers. I said, jokingly, "Let me see your hand." She had her nails painted with bright red nail polish and I said, "No wonder you don't have luck with flowers, you don't have a 'green thumb.'" We both had a good laugh over that.

This was blueberry country and we really enjoyed picking them and people gave us blueberries also. Agnes canned a lot of them for sauce. Of all the wild fruit there is, I guess blueberry sauce is my favorite. We also picked chokecherries and pin cherries for jelly.

My good friend, Morris Eggen, was pastor in a four-point parish at Shevlin, Minnesota, at the same time as I was serving in LaPorte. We were both in the Fosston District so we saw each other quite often at pastors meetings and other meetings. One of the things that often came up for discussion was the merger question. Some people in the LFC favored merger with some other Lutheran Synods and so it was brought to a referendum in 1955. It was defeated, but was brought up again in 1957 for another vote and was defeated a second time. Both Pastor Eggen and I did not feel that merger was a wise thing, as we felt many of the things emphasized by the LFC would be lost. All the churches we served voted no in the 1957 referendum. This vote was taken in November of that year.

We had a good Bible camp on the shore of Grace Lake. It was called Bethany Camp. We had both junior and senior camps for young people and the women also used it for retreats. I always promoted Bible camps wherever I served and saw much fruit in the lives of young people as well as adults.

We attended and promoted the camps of the LEM (Lutheran Evangelistic Movement). Their aim and emphasis was the same as ours which was to bring all people, young and old, into a living relationship with Jesus. The LEM summer camp was held at the campgrounds of the Mission Farms on Medicine Lake in Minneapolis during the 1950s. Their Mid-Winter Bible Conference was held in the Augustana Lutheran Church in downtown Minneapolis.

We were still very much interested in the Latin American Lutheran Mission and it's program. I was no longer treasurer as I had to give that up when we moved to Canada. We tried to attend their annual meetings as much as possible. One such meeting I attended while we lived at LaPorte was held at DeKalb, Illinois. I took a bus to Brainerd and rode with Frank Scherfenberg.

While we lived in LaPorte we were living in vacation country and we utilized it to the best advantage. We often had visitors in church on Sunday morning as there were many tourists in the area who had come from different parts of the country. I have had Governors and Senators in my audiences many times, but my message was always the same—Salvation by grace through faith in Jesus Christ to the glory of God the Father.

Chapter 22
Retirement!

Agnes and I had been thinking about our retirement, and we had been pondering where we would like to spend our declining years. Of all the places we had lived, we both liked the Spicer area. We liked the people; we liked Green Lake Lutheran Church; and of course, I liked the lakes and the good fishing. I was 68 years old and I didn't plan on taking anymore calls. In 1959, we had bought a lot from Otto Thompson in the south part of Spicer and our plan was to some day build a house on it.

Pastor Eggen and I had decided we would both retire the same year and since we both had children living in California, we decided to drive out there together and visit them. I preached my farewell sermon at LaPorte January 3, 1960. The Congregation gave us a farewell gift of $50 and Pastor Eggen gave us $75 to go toward the expenses of the trip. We drove our car and I did most of the driving. We left our furniture at LaPorte and so Pastor and Mrs. Eggen, Agnes and I left for California on January 8. Our first stop was at Pierpont, South Dakota, where we visited Agnes' mother and other relatives. The Eggens also had relatives to visit in the same area.

This was in January, so we wanted to get out of the cold as quickly as possible. We traveled south and west through Sioux Falls, South Dakota; Missouri, Kansas, New Mexico, Arizona and California. Gasoline was about 37 cents a gallon. We had a very scenic trip and enjoyed it very much. It was good to visit our children again.

Our visit in California was marred by the illness and death of Agnes' sister-in-law in Longview, Washington. Agnes spent quite a bit of the time with the family and helped care for her sister-in-law. This was a sad time for us.

Even though we were retired, we had been asked to serve Trinity Lutheran Church at Sacred Heart, Minnesota. We began our ministry there April 10, after our three months in California and Washington.

We were able to buy a good house in Sacred Heart and we got a truck to haul our furniture from LaPorte. We also hauled a lot of things in our car and trailer.

In 1958, I had sold my three lakeshore lots on Farm Island Lake and so we had this money to use to buy the house in Sacred Heart. (My father had had the lake property divided into lots and had given each of us children two lots. I had gotten a third lot from one of my brothers in payment for work I had done for him.)

Our stay in Sacred Heart was to be for only a short time, but it stretched into two and a half years. While serving in Sacred Heart we made frequent trips to Spicer, where we worked on our lot. We had a garden and berry bushes planted, also a strawberry bed. We were still planning to build on this lot and we had some estimates made, but building costs were high and seemed to be beyond our reach.

In January of 1961, we decided to make another trip to California and we were able to get our good friend Roy Carlson, a good lay speaker, to fill our pulpit in

Sacred Heart for us while we were gone. He was a member of Calvary Lutheran Church in Willmar. We spent January and February in California visiting our children and also my sister Dagny and her husband, Moselle Hilliard.

In June, we made a trip to Canada to visit Norma and family and then we all came back to Fortuna, North Dakota for the wedding of our son, Ronald, and Esther Reistad. I had the honor of officiating at their wedding. After the wedding Norma and Ed and family visited us in Sacred Heart and a few days later Tryg and Thelma and family arrived for a visit. Our house was really humming for a while with fun and good fellowship.

The members of our congregation helped us celebrate our thirty-fifth wedding anniversary in July of this same year. Our anniversary was on the eleventh but we celebrated on Sunday the eighteenth. We also celebrated my thirty-eighth year in the ministry and my 70th birthday. The congregation made it a memorable occasion for us.

While we were serving in Sacred Heart, Pastor Eggen was serving a congregation near Granite Falls. This too was on a temporary basis. Since we lived so close to each other, we were together often for visits and for times of Bible study and prayer.

Being the Eggens and we had been friends for so many years, and as Agnes and I were planning our retirement home in Spicer, Pastor Eggen was looking for a place to buy in the same area. Since I was acquainted in Spicer, having lived here before, I contacted a Christian Real Estate Agent and he took Pastor Eggen and I out and showed us several places that were for sale. One place was on the lake and there was a small cabin on the property. Eggen didn't particularly care for it as he wasn't interested in lake property, but instead he bought a house a couple miles north of Spicer.

Later on I got to thinking about that little cabin on the lakeshore lot that the real estate agent had shown to Pastor Eggen. It had a beautiful beach and I loved the lake. I had grown up on a lake—Farm Island Lake. Agnes and I looked at it again together and we gave up the idea of building on our lot and instead decided to buy this place on the lake.

We bought the lake home on Pleasantwood Beach for $8,000 from Gus Thorson and after the down payment we were to pay $50 a month, interest free. Later on we increased our payments to $100 and finally to $200 until it was paid for. Mr. and Mrs. Thorson were an older, retired couple. They surely were fine people and were good to us.

It was April 27, 1962, that we closed the deal on the property and three days later we began working on the cottage. We were still living in Sacred Heart and serving the church there, but all our spare time was spent in Spicer working on our cottage. What a joy it was for Agnes and me to go there and work. It is always fun to work on property that is your own. The cottage was just a shell, but we winterized and modernized it. We drilled a well for water and built on an addition to the house and also built a garage. This was now to be our retirement home. We planted a lot of perennials and also had a garden spot but we used our vacant lot for our main garden.

We were fortunate in that we were able to sell our house in Sacred Heart shortly after buying our lake home so we had money from that to buy things we needed for improvements on our cottage. We moved into our lake home on June 11, but continued to serve the church in Sacred Heart until fall.

The merger question in the LFC was still alive. The first two referendums had failed in 1955 an 1957. Another vote was taken in 1961, and this time it passed. The LFC as such was no more and would be merging with the ALC on February 1, 1963. Some of us pastors and many lay people were very unhappy about this decision. In many areas of the church, from time to time, people had gathered for special prayer meetings seeking God's will.

Pastor Eggen and I were two of the pastors that had voted against merger and we felt we could not, for conscience sake, go along with it. I believe it was Dr. Martin Luther who once said, "It is not good to go against conscience" and that is the way we felt. It wasn't that we felt we were better than others and we also knew that many who went into the merger were fine Christian people but we felt we must stay out.

I can remember one time the pastors of the Willmar District met at our house and in our conversation one of the pastors was trying to convince me I should go along in the merger the same as he. I told him, "No, I couldn't do that." Then he went into the kitchen and started to talk to Agnes, and tried to convince her that we should do as the rest were doing. Agnes said, "No, even if Tryg goes in, I'll have to stay out by myself." After that nothing more was said.

Our reasons for opposing the merger were not merely personal prejudices or minor differences of opinion on relatively unimportant customs and practices. Our reasons went much deeper than this; they were matters that affected our personal spiritual life and the life of the church.

Foremost, in our concern was the doctrine of the

Word of God. We believed that the entire Bible is the inspired Word of God and that it is inerrant, infallible and authoritative. Much of liberal theology was departing from this belief and was weakening the Authority of the Scriptures. We wanted to continue as a Conservative Lutheran Church.

Another concern was the new church body was a member of the World Council of Churches and we did not want to be a part of it as it seemed to favor the liberal view of theology and was not firmly grounded in the Bible as the Word of God.

Our emphasis had always been on the importance and freedom of the local congregation and we didn't want to see this change. Quoting from the *Guiding Principles of the LFC* which was written in 1897, "According to the Word of God, the Congregation is the right form of the Kingdom of God on earth."

We also felt that among Lutherans there was a place for simplicity in worship and the low-church emphasis. We believed Christianity cannot be explained, but it must be experienced and that every true Christian will live a life of personal piety. We wanted to uphold true Lutheran Pietism.

As a result of many prayer meetings and discussions in various localities by people of like mind, it was agreed to call a meeting to see how much interest there would be in forming a new church body, which would be a continuation of the Lutheran Free Church. Our Saviors Lutheran Church of Thief River Falls, Minnesota, hosted this meeting and it was held October 25–28, 1962, Thursday night through Saturday.

Pastor and Mrs. M. Eggen, Agnes and I, Pastor and Mrs. Julius Hermunslie and others from Green Lake Congregation attended this meeting in Thief River Falls.

Pastor Hermunslie was pastor of Green Lake Church at that time.

No one had any idea as to the number of people who would come. There were 23 pastors and 255 lay people registered. Some people came from other Lutheran bodies beside the LFC. The church was filled to overflowing, so on Friday afternoon the meeting was moved to the public school auditorium.

A full program had been planned for the conference consisting of devotional hours, prayer times, preaching services and business sessions. The theme of the conference was "Press on Toward the Goal" and the conference text was Philippians 3:1-16. The keynote address on Friday morning was given by Rev. John Strand speaking on the theme "The Church We Seek." Rev. Raynard Huglen read a paper on the "Historical Situation" and a statement called the "Declaration of Faith."

As a result of this conference it was voted to form an association of free and independent Lutheran Congregations adhering to the LFC "Guiding Principles." By action of the conference, we agreed to hold the first annual conference of our newly formed group in June of the following year. We elected officers who would carry on the work until then. Rev. John Strand was chosen as President, Rev. Fritjof Monseth, Vice President, and Rev. Richard Snipstead as Secretary. A Board of Administration, (this later was called the Co-Ordinating Committee) was elected with Rev. J. Hermunslie of Spicer as Chairman. Other committees were chosen to work on different areas of our endeavors together as congregations. Publication of our church paper, the *Lutheran Ambassador,* began with the first issue February 12,1963. Much had been accomplished at this conference.

The women at the conference also organized as they wanted to continue the Women's Missionary Federation. Officers were chosen to serve until conference time in June. Mrs. M. Eggen and Mrs. J. Hermunslie together with Agnes were chosen to serve on the Program Committee. Agnes was chairman of the committee.

After the conference, we had fully intended to spend the winter in our home on the lake at Spicer. We had our last service at the church in Sacred Heart in November. December 1, we drove to Pierpont, South Dakota, to visit Agnes' mother, who was ill. We also had a speaking engagement at Saron Church, Roslyn, South Dakota. While we were at Pierpont, we got a long distance call from Pukwana, South Dakota, asking us to come and serve them as interim pastor. We drove out there the following weekend, preached in both churches, met with the joint council and told them, yes, we would come and serve them. We went back to Spicer, packed up our clothes and other personal things we would need and left for Pukwana again on Thursday and took up the work there December 16.

The parsonage was right beside the church in Pukwana. We also served St. Olaf church which was ten miles out in the country. Agnes and I visited every home in both congregations the first two to three weeks we were there. We didn't stay long at each place, but we wanted to get acquainted with the people. One day we made 11 calls. We found the people to be very friendly and open to our ministry and we saw spiritual growth, especially in the rural church.

We tried to take a day or two off each week and I enjoyed fishing in the Missouri River at Chamberlain. I fished through the ice until it melted in the spring and then I fished from a boat. Fishing was good and it was a way for me to relax.

In February, we drove to McVille, North Dakota, and attended the first winter Bible Conference of our newly formed Association of Free Lutheran Congregations. I remember that trip so well, as we drove along I began humming a tune, I asked Agnes if she had ever heard that tune before and she said, "No." It was new to me, too. Agnes began humming the alto part and so we kept the melody alive in my mind all the way to McVille. That night the Lord gave me the words for the first verse and the chorus and the next night I got the other two verses. I wrote the words down and also the melody notes. I sang my new song during the last session of the Bible Conference.

I entitled my song, "The Penitent's Prayer" but later changed it to, "I Come to Thee." In the next two to three years, the Lord gave me several more songs and I had seven of them printed. Adelene did some of the harmonizing for me. I wasn't able to do that, but I could sit down to the piano and sing my songs along with my chording.

In June, we attended the First Annual Conference of our AFLC, which was held in Fargo, North Dakota. The theme of the conference was "An Open Door' taken from the text, Rev. 3:8. There were 361 lay people and 17 pastors registered. They came from many congregations. There was a spirit of optimism, hope and thankfulness to God for what He was doing among us. There were many prayer sessions as we sought God's leading. The temporary officers were all elected to full terms: President Rev. John Strand, Vice President F. Monseth, Secretary R. Snipstead. Many decisions were made.

Brazil was chosen as our mission field with Rev. John Abel as Mission Director. The conference made a recommendation that we as an AFLC establish our own seminary by the fall of 1964. (This seemed like an impossibility, but God did bring it about, so that our seminary was begun in 1964.)

The Women's Missionary Federation also met and organized. Being Agnes was chairman of the Program Committee, she was much involved with the activities of the day.

We continued to work in Pukwana. At one time, we thought we would have been done there in April, but since they hadn't been able to get a pastor, we couldn't leave them. They liked our work an didn't seem to be trying very hard to get a replacement.

A decision had been made to have a Family Bible Camp for all our churches to be held in July 1964. Agnes and I were privileged to attend this first Family Bible Camp. (This was a year of firsts.) It was held at Lake Geneva, Alexandria, Minnesota, with an attendance of over 400. The Rev. John Abel of Fargo was camp dean. It was a very good week for us. It was a time of relaxation, fellowship with friends, becoming acquainted with new friends, and most of all it was a time of enrichment through the Word of God during the Bible hours. The whole program was very gratifying.

This had been a very joyful and interesting, but extremely busy summer, which was now coming to a close. We were planning to visit our two youngest children with their families and would see two new granddaughters, whom we had not seen. They lived in western North Dakota and Canada. On the way up there we stopped at Faith, South Dakota, and attended the ordination service for Jay Erickson. I had a small part in that service. The next day we left for Elbow, Saskatchewan, where Norma and family lived. We stopped at Williston, North Dakota, and picked up Ron and Esther and their new daughter, baby Ruth. They had just come from Alaska where Ron had been stationed in the Air Force.

As we drove on our way to Canada, a little ditty came into my mind and we started singing it:

> *We're on our way to Canada, Hurrah! Hurrah!*
> *We're on our way to Canada, Hurrah! Hurrah!*
> *We're going way up North,*
> *To see our Norma's fourth,*
> *We're on our way to Canada, Hurrah! Hurrah!*

Norma's fourth was Karrie. We enjoyed being with our children and grandchildren, but it was hard for Agnes as she was suffering from a severe headache that didn't let up, but only got worse.

After arriving home, we immediately went to our doctor and he recommended we go to the University Hospital in Minneapolis as he said this was something beyond what he could take care of.

At the University Hospital they took x-rays and tests and found that she had a tumor on the brain. They wanted to do surgery and after consulting with the children we decided this was the only thing to do. Immediately after the surgery, she felt better, the headache was gone as the pressure had been relieved.

The doctor reported to us that the tumor was malignant and they were not able to remove it all as it was entwined in the brain. This was devastating news. I asked the doctor how long she would live and he said perhaps three to six months. He said there was nothing more they could do and that we should take her home and make her as comfortable as possible.

Agnes was able to leave the hospital after a week and we came home to our lake home. My sister, Borghild, who was an RN came and stayed with us and helped care for Agnes. She was a blessing, a gift from God, for both of us. We borrowed a wheelchair and in the mornings we would wheel Agnes out to the large window toward the lake and she enjoyed sitting there looking out over the lake at all the boat traffic and watching me as I worked in the flower garden around our big basswood tree.

We found much comfort in the Word of God during this trying time. We claimed Romans 14:8 as our verse. *"For whether we live, we live unto the Lord; and whether we die, we die unto the Lord: whether we live therefore, or die, we are the Lord's."* We knew God had much more in store for us in heaven than we could experience down here, as Paul says in, 1 Corinthians 2:9. *"But as it is written, Eye hath not seen, nor ear heard, neither have entered into the heart of man, the things which God hath prepared for them that love him."*

All of the children visited Mom over the Thanksgiving holiday and stayed part of the next week. We took Agnes to the hospital in Willmar on December 3. She went into a coma, but we didn't know how long that might go on and since the children needed to get back to their jobs they left for their homes early on the 6th. About noon of that same day Agnes slipped away to her heavenly home. I was able to reach all of the children, as they had stopped at relatives in South Dakota. The funeral was scheduled for Monday, but had to be postponed until Tuesday because of a bad snowstorm in South Dakota so all the roads were blocked. The children all came back for the funeral.

The day after the funeral, all the children again left

for their homes and Borghild also returned to Minneapolis. I was now alone with my sorrow and it was good to be alone. I could give vent to my grief with my tears. There is solace in tears. In the midst of sorrow there can also be joy. I rejoiced to know that Agnes had now entered eternal rest and was free from all sorrow and pain, rejoicing with her Lord and all others who had gone before her. We were still both in the same church, I in the Church Militant and she in the Church Triumphant. Her battles were over. I had the hope of seeing her again when my time would come to leave this world.

Chapter 23
Beginning Again

After Agnes' death it wasn't easy to "start over." She and I had been together 37 years and had shared joys and sorrows. We had worked together for the Lord in His church. Now I had to go on alone. Our Association of Free Lutheran Congregations was also in its infancy, so it was a new beginning for our churches too.

We had a shortage of pastors in our AFLC, and even though I was now 72 years old, my health was still good, so I offered my services as interim pastor where I was needed. I was also on the Stewardship Board and there were many invitations to speak in churches and present the work of the AFLC. I knew that Agnes would want me to continue serving the Lord to the best of my ability.

The churches at Pukwana, South Dakota, wanted me to come back there, but I felt it would be too hard as everywhere I would go I would see Agnes. She and I had gone together on visitations and she had been involved with Sunday school and WMF, so I chose rather to go to a new place.

In February of 1964, I accepted an invitation to work with the Stillwater Lutheran Congregation at Kalispell, Montana. I packed my car with my personal belongings and left my home base of Spicer and traveled across the

Dakotas and into Montana to Kalispell. As I drove along I picked up my little ditty we had sung on our way to Canada one time, but changed it to Kalispell.

I'm on my way to Kalispell, Hurrah! Hurrah!
I'm on my way to Kalispell, Hurrah! Hurrah!
I'm going way out west,
To do my very best,
To serve my Lord in Kalispell, Hurrah! Hurrah!

This congregation was a former ELC congregation that had heard about our AFLC and wanted to affiliate with us. They were about six families and there were also six families in town, some of which had been in the LFC before and preferred that fellowship. Those in town came out and joined in with those in the country. They were an enthusiastic group of people. We had Sunday school and worship services every Sunday morning. On Sunday evenings we had fellowship meetings in the homes of the members. These were precious times in the Word of God and in prayer. It was also a time of getting acquainted with each other. Some of the names I remember were the Tutvedts, Les Kjos, Oscar Olson, Lee Haag, the Maltbys and many others.

The congregation rented a house for me to live in as they had no parsonage. I suggested to the people that they build a parsonage rather than pay out rent money. They thought this was a good idea. Some of the men were carpenters, so they were able to do most of the work themselves and this helped to keep the cost down.

We could see there was much potential for growth in this area. When we had a DVBS we had a full house. The people could see that there should be a church built in town also and this came about within a short time.

While at Stillwater Lutheran, I had the joy of confirming a class of five very fine young people. They had had some instruction before and I began meeting with the class in March and confirmed them in November.

I surely enjoyed my ten months in Kalispell, and had I been younger, I could have easily made my home there. The climate was ideal. It was over the first ridge of the Rockies from the east and it was a very scenic area. The people were wonderful too.

Since I was semi-retired I would get out on the golf course occasionally with friends of mine. I had always enjoyed golfing but when I was in the full-time ministry there was never time for both and I gave up golfing in favor of the ministry. The Lord hadn't called me to be a golfer but he had called me to be a pastor.

My plan, as I left Kalispell, was to go to California and spend some time with my children. My son Olaf, who lived in southern California came to Kalispell on the bus and we continued together west and south in my car. I had written to the congregation in Everett, Washington, who had no pastor, that I would be coming through and could give them a service the following Sunday (December 6,1964). They had been served by laymen so when I came they asked if I would have a Communion service for them, to which I agreed.

After the service they wanted to give me a call immediately but I said my plans were to visit in California, but if they couldn't get anyone else by February, I would be able to come and serve them for a while. When we arrived in California, I had a letter of call waiting for me from Calvary Lutheran in Everett.

I spent a very enjoyable time with my family in California and left there February 23 and drove to Kalispell. I installed Pastor Stendal there on February 28, 1965, and took a train to Fargo, North Dakota, to attend the pastor's conference.

After getting back to Kalispell I again packed my car and was off to my new place of service in Everett, Washington.

I spent seven good months there. Our church was right in town on a corner lot. There were many fine Christian people at Calvary Lutheran. We had regular worship services and Sunday school, choir, prayer meetings, Mission Society, and we also conducted services at Bethany Home. Minnie Lande, a member of Calvary was administrator at Bethany Home. I was able to share the Word of God with many people through personal visitations.

One of my deacons who had been born and raised in that area took me around in the mountains and valleys and all places of interest. He knew all the scenic spots. He was alone, the same as I so we spent many days together driving around. We also took a few boat trips on Puget Sound.

Some of my friends were commercial fishermen and often they would bring me a salmon they had caught that day in the Sound.

I can honestly say I enjoyed every place that I served the Lord and I remember with joy the time spent in Everett.

I left there the end of September and came back to my home in Spicer. It was always good to be back in my home church, Green Lake Lutheran. My friends there were always so supportive of my ministry wherever I was, in all my travels.

The next two months I spent traveling in the interest of stewardship and visited most of our churches in central and northern Minnesota and some in North Dakota.

In 1964 the Lord enabled us to purchase a piece of

property on Medicine Lake from the Hauge Lutheran Innermission Federation. This became the permanent headquarters of our church, the Association of Free Lutheran Congregations. There was a large well-built church structure on the site which served us well. That same fall our seminary was begun with a class of ten enrolling.

Two years after the Seminary was started, the Bible school came into being. It had been talked about at every annual conference and now what had seemed to be an impossibility became a reality. The lay-people had especially wanted a Bible school so they would have a place for their young people to attend after high school where they could continue their education and become grounded in the Word of God and be better fitted for life and for service in the church, at home, or abroad, wherever the Lord would lead them. We started with 13 students the first year. There was much enthusiasm for the Bible school and the people rallied to support it. God had answered our prayers; we now had a Bible school.

In the fall of 1965, the need arose for a pastor to serve two newly formed congregations. Neither of them as yet had a church building. One was Trinity Free Lutheran in Grand Forks, North Dakota, and the other was Bethel Free Lutheran at Grafton, North Dakota.

I was asked to serve them until a permanent pastor could be secured in each place. I lived in Grand Forks and would drive to Grafton for an 8:45 A.M. service and back to Grand Forks for an 11 o'clock service.

The people were hungry for the Word of God and this was a period of growing together and becoming established in purpose. Many different personalities were being blended together into a workable unit.

I worked there the month of December and had a

confirmation service the first Sunday in January at Bethel in Grafton. That was an interesting experience. It was a class of six, and we had the service on Sunday morning but one of the members was sick and couldn't be with us. I visited her in the afternoon and she said, "Why can't you confirm me in bed?" I answered, "Yes, I will do that." So with her parents as an audience, I asked her the same questions as I had asked the rest of the class earlier in the day and I confirmed her in bed. This was a very meaningful experience for all of us, especially for me. This was a first in my life as a pastor.

Before going to Grand Forks and Grafton my plans had been to spend some time in January and February with my son Trygve Jr. and family who was living in Roy, Utah, at the time. So the day after this confirmation service I proceeded with those plans and drove to Spicer and later on west to Utah. After leaving there the latter part of February, I visited a few days in Minneapolis and St. Paul with some of my brothers and sisters and two of my children.

I returned to Grand Forks on March 1, and took up the work there again. We had a Lenten Service there that night and the following night we had a Lenten Service at Bethel in Grafton. After the service it was snowing heavily so I was invited to stay overnight at Herb Presteng's. The wind had come up so it would have been impossible to drive back to Grand Forks that night. The blizzard continued for two more days and the local people said it was the worst blizzard they had had in 50 years. After the blizzard quieted down we walked out and there were places the drifts were over the telephone lines so we could actually walk across them. During the blizzard we couldn't get off the place so we had a lot of time to relax, visit, read and enjoy Mrs. Presteng's good cooking.

While I was serving these two congregations they both voted to build churches as soon as they were able. On June 26, 1966, Bethel Free Lutheran in Grafton had groundbreaking ceremonies at the site of their new church. I was privileged to have a part in this service and had the honor of turning the first shovel full of dirt. They built their church that summer and the congregation in Grand Forks built theirs a year later.

My last service in this parish was July 24. The congregations had been able to secure the services of seminarian, David Molstre. I therefore was no longer needed.

I was driving a 1965 Ford Falcon at this time and I really put the miles on it. It served me well. After leaving Grand Forks I attended our Family Bible Camp at Lake Geneva, Alexandria, Minnesota; then there was a quick trip to Canada for the 60th anniversary of Skudesnes Congregation and also to visit my daughter and family, the Ed Knutsons at Elbow, Saskatchewan. Besides this I had invitations to speak in several churches to bring a message from the Word of God and to speak on behalf of stewardship in our churches. Every year in June was annual conference time and this year it was in Thief River Falls, Minnesota. I was kept very busy.

This was a sad year too. Two of my brothers passed away, Anker on June 9, and Viggo on August 29. They both had served their Lord well as pastors and now they were called to their heavenly home.

I had only been free for about a month and a half when I was asked to go to Fargo and begin serving St. Paul's Lutheran Church. My first service there was September 18, 1966. One of my good friends there was

Gus Arneson. He had the same birthday as I, only he was a year older. There were many fine Christians in this congregation—Joe Solbergs, Nels Floms, and Russell Duncan, to mention a few. It was good to see the spiritual as well as numerical growth of the congregation. For a while we had a radio program on a local station. I had been elected to the Mission Board of the AFLC at an annual conference so often the board would come to Fargo for our monthly meetings. There were many decisions to make, so we spent much time in discussion and in prayer.

St. Paul's congregation hosted the 1967 annual conference in June and we were able to use the facilities of Oak Grove Lutheran High School. We had dormitories, cafeteria and conference rooms, so it served us well.

One of the main items of business at the 1967 conference was discussion concerning the need for a dormitory/classroom building to be built at our headquarters property on Medicine Lake. This was an urgent need. We had begun our Bible school in the fall of 1966 and by doing some minor remodeling we had dormitory rooms, classrooms, offices and eating facilities all in our main building. As the enrollment grew our concern was to have a girls dormitory.

Definite plans were made to have a special financial project for the new dormitory. This was called "One Grand Fellowship" and was to consist of $1,000 gifts from individuals. The response was enthusiastic by those at the conference and several responded with gifts or pledges of $1,000 immediately.

I was engaged by the conference to travel and visit our churches and receive $1,000 gifts from our constituents. I was through as a pastor now at St. Paul's of Fargo so I gladly accepted this challenge. I was totally convinced of the value of our Bible school and saw the great need for a dormitory/classroom building so it wasn't hard for me to present the work to our people.

I traveled that fall and part of the next year and visited our churches in the Midwest besides those in Upper Michigan and on the West Coast. In the fall of 1967, after being in the churches in Washington, I traveled down the coast to San Bernardino in Southern California and there I officiated at the wedding of my son Olaf and Susan Charboneau on December 9. At the same time I visited other relatives in California.

The response in our church to the "One Grand Fellowship" was very encouraging. One man said that I had taught him how to give joyfully to the Kingdom work. One lady pledged $1,000 on the condition that God would give her a job, which He did, and she was able to fulfill her pledge. She received much joy through this experience.

Through the funds received from the "One Grand Fellowship," other gifts, and loans, we were able to have groundbreaking ceremonies for the new building March 27, 1968, and it was ready for occupancy that fall. What a blessing this building has proved to be. The people had given their support so joyfully we could all rejoice together at its dedication in June of 1969.

These were very busy years for me even though I was "retired." I continued to accept invitations to speak in our churches. Sometimes I had more invitations than I could fulfill, so I had to use my own judgment as to which place I could serve best.

I tried to spend some of the coldest part of the winter almost each year in California with my children. My home on Green Lake was on the southeast corner of the lake. When there was a northwest wind, the snow would really pile in there, almost covering the house. I remember one winter I tunneled from the back door of the house to the back door of the garage.

This same winter, one time when I was snowed in and the power was off, so I had no heat. I was listening to my battery operated radio and the announcer said that if anyone was snowed in there were some fellows with snowmobiles that would help. I called them and they came out and they went to the front door first, but there was so much snow there they went to the back door and shoveled so I could get out. I rode to town with them on the snowmobile.

Pastor Julius Hermunslie, who had served Green Lake Lutheran for many years resigned and had his farewell sermon on November 17, 1968. During this time of pastoral vacancy I served my home church. Pastor Galland was called and began serving us September 7, 1969.

My sister, Borghild Dahle, was in failing health. She had lived some with relatives in Minneapolis and also for a short time with a sister in California. She had stayed with me here at Spicer from time to time. I had told her as long as I had a home, she would have a home. The time came when she required more care than I could give her and so she entered Bethesda Country Home in April of 1969, and later she was transferred to the Bethesda Home in Willmar. She passed away March 30, 1974.

During these years when I was traveling so much I always managed to get back to my home in Spicer from time to time, and the first thing I did was mow my lawn and go through my garden with the cultivator. I enjoyed my garden and flowers.

Two summers I called my garden my "mission garden." I sold the surplus of my berries and vegetables to the summer resorters around the lake. All the proceeds of these sales I gave to missions. God blessed my garden and it produced well. The lake people were happy to get fresh vegetables out of the garden so I had no trouble getting customers.

In March of 1972, Pastor Strand, President of our AFLC, asked me to go and serve interim at Boscobel, Wisconsin. I was there three months and then left to attend the annual conference. I would have gone back after the conference but I had previous appointments which I had to fulfill. The church at Boscobel was able to secure the services of a seminarian.

That fall I had surgery at Veteran's Hospital in Minneapolis and after recovering, Pastor Strand asked me to go to the Tioga Parish and serve until they could get a pastor. There were four churches in this parish, which kept me very busy. I was assisted by a local layman, Rodger Olson. I asked him to take care of the young people's activities and I would take care of the other duties. I told him that even though I was the Senior Pastor and he was my assistant, I felt it should really be reversed. He should be called the Senior Pastor and I his assistant. I was at the end of my years as a pastor and he was just beginning. He served me well as a layman and later entered the seminary and was ordained. We each preached in two churches each Sunday.

The 1973 annual conference was at Ferndale, Washington. A good friend of mine from the parish was going, and he offered me a ride. We had a good trip and a good time of fellowship as we traveled to the coast. After a very enjoyable conference, we made the return trip to Tioga through Canada.

I enjoyed my time of service in Tioga immensely. The people in this parish were some of the finest I have ever served in all my ministry. They were very kind to me. I completed 50 years in the ministry while serving this parish and they honored me by hosting an open house for me. This was on June 24 and it was also my last Sunday there. Rev. Forrest Swenson had accepted their call and had come to serve them.

In these 50 years I had served in 16 parishes with 37 congregations and preaching places. Tioga was the last place I served as interim pastor.

For some time I had had a desire to visit my relatives in Norway. All my aunts and uncles on both Father's and Mother's sides had passed away, but I still had many cousins and second cousins living there. After finishing my work in the Tioga Parish I had sufficient funds to make the trip.

I left Minneapolis July 29, at 1:25 P.M. and flew to New York, changed planes and arrived at Oslo, Norway the next morning at 9:40 A.M. I spent six very enjoyable weeks in Norway getting acquainted with my cousins, whose names I knew, but I had never met any of them except one, Thor Wangen, who had visited in the USA, the year previous. Mother's relatives lived on the east side of Norway near the Swedish border at Magnor and Father's people were in the west part of Norway near Volda. My cousin, Thor, took me by car from Magnor to Volda. We traveled up Gulbrandsdalen and across the mountains, which was a very scenic area. There was snow in the mountains where we crossed and this was in August.

My relatives were surprised that I could speak such good Norwegian. They could all understand me and of course I spoke the "Old Norwegian" which I had learned from Dad and Mother. The "New Norsk" and the dialects I knew nothing about, even though I could understand most of them, but I couldn't speak them.

Besides visiting my relatives, I spent a week in Stavanger visiting Agnes' uncle and an aunt. I had many interesting experiences while in Norway, one of which was to spend a week at a Bible camp for "Eldre Folk" or as we would say for senior citizens. I had the privilege of speaking at that camp. I also went with my cousin Ruth Gausteseter to a Sunday school teacher's institute and I took part in several home Bible studies and prayer groups among some of my relatives. I was very pleased to find so many of my cousins who were truly Bible believing, confessing Christians. All in all my visit to Norway was a memorable time in my life.

Chapter 24
No Longer Alone

After being alone for 11 years, God was good to me. God answered my prayers and gave me another helpmate. We had met at the annual conference in Cloquet, Minnesota, and had gotten better acquainted the three months I served Anna's church in Wisconsin. As time went on, both of us felt that God was leading us to spend our lives together.

We decided on a simple service and were married following the morning service on Sunday, May 11, 1975. We were married in Anna's home church, Trinity Lutheran at Boscobel, Wisconsin, by Pastor Frank Miller. Following the ceremony we had a lovely dinner reception at the church. Three of my children attended our wedding: Marjorie and her husband, Gene Zugschwert; Ronald, who also served as my best man, and his wife Esther and their two children; and Norma, who surprised us and came from Canada.

On Tuesday evening, Gene and Marjorie gave us a reception at their home in St. Paul. What a wonderful occasion this was. There were about 70 guests, my relatives, Anna's relatives, and our friends who lived in the Twin Cities area. We both got acquainted with each others relatives and friends.

I had purchased tickets for us on a chartered flight to Norway. It was a three-week trip, but after arriving in

Norway we were free to go wherever we wanted to. We left the Minneapolis airport on May 15, at 8 A.M. and flew non-stop to Oslo, arriving about 10:15 P.M., Norway time. It was an eight hour flight but there is a time change of about six hours. This was the first time Anna had flown but she enjoyed it. We flew over Hudson Bay, Greenland, and Iceland to Oslo. As we flew over Greenland, it seemed as though we could have almost reached out our hand and touched the highest peaks of the mountains. Our plane was a Finnish plane, called the Finnair. We had a smooth flight.

We stayed our first night in Norway at the Norrena Hotel, which is operated by one of the mission societies of Norway. Breakfast was included in our night's lodging and what a breakfast. It was a real smorgasbord—cheeses, fish, eggs, cereal, fruit, and much more. That same day we took a train to Magnor, which is on the east side of Norway near the Swedish border, where we stayed four days with Bjarne and Ruth (Gaustester) Bjornstad. Ruth had married since I visited there in 1973. Ruth's father was my cousin on my mother's side.

We were at Magnor for the "Syttende Mai" celebration, which is Norway's Independence Day, May 17. This is a very festive time. Many of the ladies wear their special Norwegian costume. These dresses have intricate embroidery and are very beautiful. Each locality in Norway has its distinct design. May 17, was on a Saturday and it began with a service in the church, then a parade with the school children and bands, a program at the school, and another service in the church in the evening.

On Sunday the 18th, which was Pentecost Sunday we attended services at Eidskog Church. Many of my relatives were at this service. Monday was the Second

Day of Pentecost and the working people had this day as a holiday. There was a service in the Magnor Chapel on Second Day of Pentecost and I had the privilege to preach the sermon. It was such a joy to meet so many of my relatives. We had two more days in Magnor and on Wednesday night, we had a "vennemate" at Ruth and Bjarnes. That was what we would call a fellowship meeting, with Bible readings, prayers, and a time of sharing. Bjarne played an accordion, so there was singing too. What a blessed time we had at Magnor.

Our next place to visit was Hedalen in Valdres, which is northwest of Oslo. We took a train again from Magnor back to Oslo and then a bus to Hedalen. Anna's ancestors all came from this part of Norway. We stayed with Mr. and Mrs. Per Goplerud, who as nearly as we can determine, was a fifth cousin of Anna's. They lived up in the mountains. We saw the old Hedalen "Stave-Kirke" which had been built in 1150, rebuilt in 1738, and restored again in 1901. There were many very old furnishings in this church; one was the cover for the baptismal font, which was made of copper. The year 1702 was engraved on it and it was a work of art. We were told it had been made by one of Anna's ancestors. The pillars and door casings were wooden and had intricate and complex carvings covering the entire surface. There wasn't any worship service in this church the Sunday we were there but we did attend a little Sunday school that was conducted in the "Bedehus." After the service, we found out that the couple leading the service were distant relatives of Anna's. We saw the farm where her grandmother was born and it is still occupied by relatives. The old "Stabur" was still on the place but was no longer being used. The State Churches are kept up by the government, but the "Bedehus" or prayer houses are built and maintained by the people.

We left Hedalen and went back to Oslo by bus, then got on a train and traveled all day around the southern tip of Norway to Stavanger. This was a unique experience. We went through 187 tunnels. This was really a scenic trip. We spent two days in Stavanger and visited the 90-year-old uncle of Agnes, my first wife. He treated us royally and we enjoyed out time there.

At Stavanger we got a plane and flew to Alesund in the northern part of Norway. Here we were to visit my father's people. Arnfinn Rangseter met us and he took us by car and ferry to his place for supper. Then we went to another second cousin, Rasmus and Signe Nautvik, who lived at Dalsfjord close to Volda and Folkestad. We were there nine days. Rasmus, who worked in blacktopping of roads, took off work and spent all his time with us. He took us to a different place of scenic beauty every day and we visited many, many relatives. We saw the beautiful fjords and mountains and traveled much on ferries, getting from one place to another. It was interesting to see the homes nestled at the foot of the mountains on a little strip of land next to the fjords.

On Sunday we worshiped in the Dalsfjord Church and I had the joy of preaching the sermon. It was all in Norwegian, of course. Most of our relatives couldn't speak English. Anna's Norwegian came back to her too, so she managed very well. I teased her and said she was speaking Valdres, not Norwegian! Each place in Norway has their own dialect.

It was soon time for us to leave Norway; we again traveled by bus and train to Oslo. Norway has good public transportation. There seem to be trains and buses everywhere. We spent two more nights in Oslo and then flew back home to the USA. We left Norway at midnight and got to the Twin Cities at 2:15 A.M. We gained six hours because of the different time zones. After getting through customs, we drove home to Spicer. Marjorie and Gene had brought our car to the airport. We arrived in Spicer just as the sun was rising. This was the first we had been to Spicer since we were married.

I had sold my lake home and bought a house in town about a year before Anna and I were married. Now the "brown house right beside the water tower" was to be our home together. There wasn't much time to settle down yet, as this was a year of much travel for us.

We were only home a day and just had time to mow the lawn, wash some clothes, and repack a suitcase and then drove to Minneapolis, where the annual conference of our church was held that year. We had been assigned a room in the new boys dormitory and someone had put a sign on the door, "Honeymoon Suite." We don't know who was responsible for the sign but someone evidently had a good time doing it and it became the cause for a lot of good humor.

One of the highlights of this conference was the dedication of the boys dormitory. It had been built in 1974. We now had two dormitories besides the main building on our headquarters property, so the facilities were adequate for the time being.

On Sunday afternoon, after the conference closed, we again drove home to Spicer. Monday was spent getting ready for a trip to California.

We were in California two weeks. I was eager to introduce Anna to my three children and their families, who lived in California and also to my sister and her husband. The first Sunday we were there Trygve Jr. and his wife Thelma had arranged a lovely open house reception for us with relatives and friends—about 55 people. The second Sunday, Olaf and Susie hosted an open house in honor of Trygve Jr. and Thelma's silver wedding anniversary. During the two weeks we were in California my children took us to visit many of the points of interest, some of which I had seen before, but it was all new for Anna as it was her first trip to California. Anna enjoyed seeing the different kinds of trees and shrubs which we don't have in the Midwest. She also got to see the vast Pacific Ocean. All in all our stay in California was very pleasant and enjoyable.

After we came home from California, we were home just a day and a half and then drove to the family Bible camp at Galilee Bible Camp, Lake Bronson, Minnesota. This was the first year the family camp had been held there. This was almost like coming home for me as I had spent several years of my early ministry in this area of northern Minnesota. We got to see many of my former parishioners and I was happy to be able to introduce them to Anna. Camp was a real relaxing time for us after all our traveling since we were married.

The ladies in our home church in Spicer had been wanting to welcome us with an open house reception ever since our wedding, but we were never home long enough so they could accomplish this! We were home most of July and August so on August 3, they were finally able to fulfill their plans and gave us a wonderful reception. As always, they made it into a real festive event. Anna felt right at home with the ladies in Green Lake Church.

Our pastor at Green Lake, Les Galland, had taken a call to Calvary Lutheran at Everett, Washington, so I was asked to help out during the time we were without a pastor, which I did for those two months; however, we had plans to go to Wisconsin in September.

We hadn't been back to Anna's home since our wedding in May. I had promised to preach for the pastor in Boscobel while he was on vacation and also had scheduled special meetings in the country church, Hickory Grove Lutheran.

Being we had two homes, we had to dispose of one of them and since Anna had no immediate family anymore in Boscobel, we decided to make our home in Spicer. We prepared to have an auction sale and dispose of surplus things and made arrangements to sell Anna's house. It was a beautiful, warm, sunny day the day of our sale and we got to see many friends and relatives. After a very busy month in Wisconsin and after the auction we packed a U-Haul trailer with things we wanted to bring with us to my home in Spicer, which we now had decided to make our home. A friend of ours came to Wisconsin and drove my Maverick back to Spicer and we had a trailer hitch put on Anna's car and hauled our own things in the U-Haul.

When we got back to Spicer, my home congregation wanted me to continue serving until we could get a pastor, but I felt the load would be too heavy at my age. We were also serving Zion Church in Willmar and I thought responsibility of two congregations would be too much, especially with winter coming on, so instead the congregations engaged a seminarian.

In the middle of November we made a trip to Ortley, South Dakota, where I had a series of meetings in Ortley Free Lutheran Church. Einar Unseth was the pastor. We had very good meetings with good attendance and a fine spirit in spite of a severe snowstorm which we could have called a "near blizzard." When we were ready to come home we called a friend in Spicer and asked how the weather was. He said, "You'd better stay where you are until the weather settles. We've had 17 inches of snow and the roads are blocked." We stayed another day and drove home, but in some places there was only one lane of the road open and we had a lot of shoveling to do to get the car in the garage.

We surely had a busy year this first year of our marriage. We had done so much traveling. I think Anna thought it was almost too much, but she enjoyed it and we survived.

For a long time, I had had a desire to visit our mission field in Brazil, but I never thought it would materialize until one day we got a letter from Pastor John Abel telling us he was organizing a tour to Brazil. We felt if we were to see our mission field it would have to be now, so we accepted and made our plans.

We left the Minneapolis airport on February 23,1976, on Northwest Airlines and flew to Miami, Florida, changed to Pan-AM, and made a stop in Panama and on to Rio De Janeiro. It was 79 degrees when we landed in Rio.

We were in Brazil two weeks. The first week was spent sightseeing in Rio, and São Paulo. We also saw the magnificent Iguacu Falls and made a short trip into Argentina and Paraguay. We saw the markers where the three countries come together. We stayed in nice hotels, and with Pastor Abel along to do our talking for us, it all went well. Many things were different than in the USA. We were served by waiters instead of waitresses. We bought our drinking water in bottles until we got to the mission compound. There the water was safe to drink as there is a good well there. We saw coffee trees growing and saw a variety of farming methods—some were tilling the soil with a hoe and we also saw many modern tractors.

A Pioneer Church Family

We left Foz do Iguacu by bus to go to Campo Mourao. It was about 160 miles and part of the way it was good blacktop, but we also had many miles of rough dirt road to travel on. The soil is red in color so there was a thick cloud of red dust behind the bus as we traveled, and we were enveloped by it when we met another vehicle.

We were glad to get to the mission and Connely and Carolyn Dyrud took good care of us. Here we didn't need to worry about eating something that would make us sick and we had good drinking water. It was good to see the grounds here at the Bible school, girls dorm, boys dorm, dining room, chapel room, nice lawn and garden area.

We saw the two churches in town, Lar Parana and the Central Church and also were in three other churches, several miles away: Alvorada, Iretama, and Umuarama. We attended services in some of them. We didn't understand the language but we could sense the sincerity and warm-heartedness of the Christians as they shared Scripture and prayed. We had meals in some of their homes and they freely shared what they had. Rice and beans were always served and we often got chicken or some other meat and different kinds of fruit.

This part of Brazil had been all jungle until 1945 when it was opened up, so it was still in a pioneer stage, but they have come a long way and are gradually getting hard surface roads. There was much building going on. It was summer while we were there and it was very hot—in the 90s and even up to 100 degrees at times.

It was such a joy to see what our mission dollars had accomplished and now when we hear our missionaries talk about the various places in the field, we know what they're talking about, because we have been there.

We took many snapshots and slides in Brazil and so when we showed our pictures, after our return, people could visualize the work on the field and get a better understanding of the work we were supporting. That summer and fall we were able to visit many of our churches, show our slides, and present the work of World Missions.

In the summer of 1976, we visited my daughter Norma in Elbow, Saskatchewan, Canada, and Anna got to meet Norma's family, the Knutsons. We also drove to Alberta, Canada, and visited Anna's relatives in Sundre and the Camrose area.

I had very much enjoyed the time I had spent in the churches on the west coast and I had a real longing in my heart to see those people once more. I was reminded of the words of the Apostle Paul when he spoke to Barnabas in Acts 15:36 *"...Let us go again and visit our brethren in every city where we have preached the word of the Lord, and see how they do."* So in February of 1978, we bought one-way train tickets to Los Angeles, California, with several stopovers. We boarded the train in Willmar, Minnesota, and traveled via Amtrak. Both Anna and I enjoyed traveling by rail.

Our first stop was at Whitefish, Montana, where we were met by Pastor John Rieth. We spent the weekend at Kalispell and I had the joy to speak both in Stillwater Lutheran, where I had served and in Faith Free in Kalispell, which was built after I left there.

Our next stop was Seattle where we were guests of Pastor and Mrs. Les Galland. We were able to bring a message from the Lord again in Calvary at Everett; Triumph at Ferndale, where we visited Pastor and Mrs. Richard Snipstead; and Elim at Lake Stevens. It warmed my heart to see how the Christians had advanced spiritually in their walk with the Lord, and had also grown numerically since we had last seen them.

As we traveled on the train, at times the view of the mountains was spectacular. We got to Longview, Washington, on a Tuesday afternoon and spent an enjoyable evening with two sisters of my first wife, Agnes.

We boarded the train again on Wednesday and were met by Pastor Stephen Odegaard at Eugene, Oregon. We were to speak that night at the church he was serving, Spencer Creek, but we were afraid we wouldn't make it in time as the train was late. We had some anxious moments but it worked out so we did arrive in time for the service. The next day, Pastor and Mrs. Odegaard took us to visit Pastor Lars Stalsbroten at Woodburn, Oregon. He was the oldest Pastor in the AFLC at that time.

Another stop was at San Jose, California, where we visited Mr. and Mrs. Norman Rehbein. Mrs. Rehbein is the daughter of my good friends, the late Pastor and Mrs. Morris Eggen.

Our last stop was Los Angeles where Trygve Jr. and his wife Thelma met us at the depot and took us to their home in Westminster. We spent the month of March in sunny California and enjoyed the warmer climate which was different than Minnesota. We were able to visit all our family in California. On Easter Sunday, March 26, after going to church with my youngster sister, Dagny and her husband Moselle Hilliard, we had a family gathering for dinner at their home in Oceanside, California. We rode back to Westminster with Trygve Jr. and Thelma and a couple of days later they took us to the Orange County Airport where we boarded a plane and flew to Phoenix, Arizona.

We visited a couple of days in Mesa with a friend of Anna's and then took a bus to Nogales, Arizona. I wanted Anna to see the work being done by Pastor and Mrs. Lawrence Dynneson and Mr. and Mrs. Leonard Swanson at Triumph Lutheran Church. I had been to Nogales before.

As we traveled south on the bus we noticed a change in the countrywide. Of special note were the huge upright cacti like men standing with outstretched arms. There was also a difference in the passengers getting on the bus. At Tucson we changed bus drivers and the new driver was Spanish speaking. From there to Nogales we heard almost more Spanish than English. That was true of Nogales, as well.

We had three delightful days in Nogales with Pastor and Mrs. Dynneson as our host. The first evening, there was a WMF meeting in the church with about 20 ladies. The business meeting and Bible study were conducted in the English language, but a lady immediately translated it into Spanish for the benefit of those who didn't know the English, so we heard two languages being spoken at the same time. It was a very interesting evening and we sensed the warm spiritual atmosphere of the group.

The following day Pastor Dynneson took us into Mexico, where we saw the poverty and poor living conditions for some of the people. The roads and streets were rough and hilly so it was hard on his car. He drove in low gear so much that it caused his car to overheat. We stopped at a home where he was acquainted and got some water for the radiator.

On Sunday we had the joy of worshipping in Triumph Lutheran Church. There again the service was in English and the Spanish speaking people sat in a group and a lady translated for them.

We had our Sunday dinner at the Dynnesons, together with the Swansons and Pastor and Mrs. Gerald Mundfrom. These three families all lived on the grounds and we each contributed something to the dinner. It was a time of rich fellowship.

The next day we took the bus back to Phoenix, visited in Mesa and Sun City and flew home to Minnesota. We had spent two rich and enjoyable months in our travels.

It was good to be home again to our "little brown house right beside the water tower," and to be with our friends at home once more.

In 1981, Anna, with the assistance of some of the ladies from church hosted an open house for me for my ninetieth birthday. Five of my children and fifteen of my grandchildren were with us besides other relatives and friends. It was truly a wonderful day—a day to remember.

Ten years before this, the ladies of the church had a party for me when I was 80 years old. That seemed old at that time, and I never thought I would reach 90 but by the grace of God I did, and have gone beyond that now. Each day is a gift from God for which we thank and praise him and he alone knows the number of our days—all He expects of us is that we are ready to answer His call. Thanks be to God.

Chapter 25
Conclusion—In Retrospect

As I look back on my life, I can only say, God has been good to me. I am thankful—that I was born into a Christian home. I never heard my father and mother quarrel. We had a peaceful home and they lived Christ before us children, so that I never knew a time when I didn't believe in Jesus as my personal Savior.

I am thankful—God called me into the ministry. I had felt a gentle call, from the Lord, from my early childhood to be a pastor, and I've never been sorry I said, "Yes," to His call. If I had my life to live over again, I would do the same.

I am thankful—for my wife, Agnes and how she always stood with me in everything and also for our six children, who even though we had very limited means to live on they never complained but were content with what we could give them. We had a closely knit family.

I am thankful—also for my second wife, Anna who came into my life several years after Agnes' death. She fit into the family so beautifully and has been a great blessing to us all.

I am thankful—how God has protected me in my extensive travels. He even protected me from some thugs that robbed me in the bus depot in Winnipeg, Canada, one time. Another time He protected me when

I fell asleep at the wheel and went off the road in a coulee. If I would have continued on I would have hit a concrete abutment and been killed, but instead, God woke me up in time and I was able to get back on the road with no harm either to me or the car. Nothing can happen to a child of God without the Lord's permission.

I am thankful—for my many Christian friends far and near, who have continually followed me in their prayers.

I am thankful—most of all, for the grace of God which has been with me from childhood. It is by grace we have been saved and it is by grace we are kept day by day and by grace we will enter the place He has prepared for us and will be with Him forever. A few of my favorite Bible verses which I have quoted hundreds of times in my messages are: Ephesians 2:8–9, John 6:37, I John 1:9, and Isaiah 43:25.

God has been good to me all my life and used me in his service in many places, and I am looking forward to the time when I can thank Him personally and see the place He has prepared for me. *"...I go to prepare a place for you. And if I go and prepare a place for you, I will come again, and receive you unto myself; that where I am, there ye may be also."* (John 14:2–3). Amen. See you there.

"My God, How wonderful thou art,
Thou everlasting Friend!
On Thee I stay my trusting heart,
'Til faith in vision end."